Intercultural Resource Pack

Intercultural communication resources for language teachers

Derek Utley

CAMBRIDGE
UNIVERSITY PRESS

CAMBRIDGE UNIVERSITY PRESS
Cambridge, New York, Melbourne, Madrid, Cape Town, Singapore,
São Paulo, Delhi, Dubai, Tokyo, Mexico City

Cambridge University Press
The Edinburgh Building, Cambridge CB2 8RU, UK

www.cambridge.org
Information on this title: www.cambridge.org/9780521533409

First published 2004
7th printing 2011

Printed in the United Kingdom by Short Run Press, Exeter

A catalogue record for this publication is available from the British Library

ISBN 978-0-521-53340-9 Book

Contents

Thanks and acknowledgements

Derek Utley wrote the original *Culture Pack* for York Associates in 2000. Not only does York Associates owe him an unpayable debt for his work as a partner in the company for more than 20 years, but also for the time, effort and dedication which he has so typically given to this project. Derek is not just a creative materials writer. His commitment to international communication has been lifelong and his character is proof of the richness of its benefits.

York Associates would also like to thank James R. Chamberlain, Director of the Language Centre of the Bonn-Rhein-Sieg University of Applied Sciences, Germany. Jim possesses the special talent of being able to convert his extensive knowledge of this subject into stimulating training tools that engage the widest possible range of user. We are very grateful to him for the Introduction to Intercultural Studies; for providing the Recommended reading list; for the Further reading references which appear in each set of Teacher's notes; and for the Background briefings.

Steve Flinders, York Associates
www.york-associates.co.uk

Publisher's acknowledgements

The author and publisher would like to thank Alison Silver for her expert editorial guidance on this project.

The publisher would also like to thank George Tomaszewski, Transfer Conseil Formation, France and Norman Frank Whitby, UK for their help in reviewing the material and for the invaluable feedback they provided.

Every effort has been made by the publisher to gain permission for all copyright material used. In the cases where this has not been possible, copyright holders are encouraged to contact the publisher.

The material about the Hofstede model on pages 62 and 63 is reproduced with permission of Professor Geert Hofstede; the material by Fons Trompenaars on page 65 is reproduced with permission of the McGraw-Hill Companies; the material about the Mole model on page 67 is reproduced with permission of Nicholas Brealey.

About this pack

Why intercultural?

Intercultural communication has been a vital issue since the world began. Intercultural competence can end disputes, save lives, radically transform the existence of millions of people; it can lubricate the wheels of industry and business; it can help teams win, whether they be sports teams or teams of international aid workers.

No wonder, then, that as the globalisation (see activities 1.6 and 1.7) of business and leisure propels international contact forward at a dizzy rate, 'international communication' is a phrase heard more and more often in the worlds of business, education and training. Understanding and optimising it is as vital to survival as it is fashionable.

The terms 'intercultural', 'cross-cultural' and 'multicultural' are referred to in the Introduction to Intercultural Studies (page 7).

The purpose of these materials

The Intercultural Resource Pack gathers together the best of current thinking and practice, and forms a set of materials which are easily accessible to and usable by teachers, trainers and others responsible for personnel development. They can be used as seminar and discussion material, and to support presentations on intercultural communication.

Contents

The pack consists of:
- an Introduction by James R. Chamberlain, of the Bonn-Rhein-Sieg University of Applied Sciences near Bonn, Germany, who has integrated intercultural communication work into an innovative programme for his German students in higher education
- a set of photocopiable activities consisting of discussion topics, exercises and explanations
- teacher's notes for each activity including, where appropriate, possible outcomes
- recommendations for further reading for those who wish to study the subject more deeply.

Format of the materials

The spiral-bound format allows photocopying of the activities for use as handouts or transparencies. The activities are divided into sections and consist of information, opinions and short texts presented in such a way as to invite discussion and group activity. They are designed to be modular: any activity can be used independently of the others.

How to use this pack

1 The materials follow no specific school of thought. Instead, they embrace and introduce a number of current approaches and theories on intercultural communication, and make them available for teachers and students to use as desired.

2 The learning style adopted is experiential, based on the principle that people in a training or educational setting learn better by carrying out activities than by being passive. Within this loose framework, teachers are encouraged to use the materials in the way best suited to their style and their students' styles.

3 Many of the activities are provocative; none is meant to be outrageous. Certain views and opinions are presented which are certainly held by some percentage of the population, but will not necessarily be held by a majority of any group of participants.

4 Most of the activities will be best done as follows: a short explanation, division into pairs or groups for discussion, then feedback and discussion in the main group.

5 The main role of the teacher is to present the activities, and then to mediate and channel the mental and nervous energy they will almost certainly generate. The questions posed are not trick questions, nor will they have one 'correct' answer. The possible outcomes in the Teacher's notes will give some guidance where necessary.

It may sometimes be useful to stimulate further discussion through questioning and redefining certain ideas. The Teacher's notes give some suggestions.

Basic assumptions about cultural development

A distinction is made between two different kinds of intercultural development:
- intercultural awareness or sensitisation – being aware of the existence of a number of different cultures and types of culture, and of their importance in all forms of human interaction, in private and working life; and
- cultural briefing – acquiring information about how particular cultures operate and manifest themselves.

The assumption is also made that intercultural competence consists of two main elements:
- cultural knowledge – understanding cultural differences, both factual and affective; and
- cultural skills – the ability to act and react in a variety of cultures, and to put this interaction to good effect. These skills include attitudes of openness and tolerance, and the ability to cope with ambiguity.

Further development

Teachers are encouraged to add to these materials from their own experience; to include items and observations from students; and to develop networking with other teachers in order to benefit from their varied experience.

An Introduction to Intercultural Studies

by James R. Chamberlain

A cultural anecdote

Twenty years ago I moved from a small town in the American Midwest to Stuttgart, Germany. I clearly remember my first day in the city: it was a sunny spring day and I was full of the promise and excitement of new adventure. As I strolled down the main shopping street, passers-by would catch my eye, and of course I greeted them with a hearty 'Guten Tag!' Not to do so would have been rude. In fact, where I come from, making eye contact with other people obliges one to acknowledge their status as a fellow human being with a hi, a hello, or a nod and a smile.

But the Stuttgarters didn't return my greeting. Most of them ignored me; some gave me what seemed to be bemused, perhaps condescending smiles; and a few stopped in their tracks, looked at me and scratched their heads as if to say, 'Do I know that guy?'

I soon learned that German city dwellers don't usually greet strangers on the street, although they'll look you up and down and straight in the eye. And yet, after twenty years in this country, I still have to repress the urge to say hello when I make eye contact with someone on the street, and deep down I'm a little disappointed that they don't want to greet me. I try not to hold it against them.

It is a long and often arduous journey from the natural state of believing that the way we do things at home is the only right way, to the learned state of accepting foreign ways as neither better nor worse, but just different. And happy the person whose path is made a bit smoother by that judicious bit of knowledge, advice or instruction. For all the importance that intercultural communication in recent years has gained – in business and industry, in politics and diplomacy, in tourism and travel – it is still at its core a basic human problem: how to cope with displacement, with being a stranger in a strange land.

Forewarned is forearmed, and those who prepare others for sojourns abroad, or help to ease visitors into their new and unaccustomed surroundings, are providing a truly human service. But trainers need preparation too, and Derek Utley offers here invaluable assistance in the form of photocopiable activities for intercultural communication training. The modular design of *The Intercultural Resource Pack* allows trainers to construct a program that leads their students through a process of guided discovery, from increased knowledge of other cultures (and hence their own), to heightened sensitivity to other value systems, whether these be in faraway lands or in one's next-door neighbor. This process in turn fosters openness, tolerance and acceptance, which help us meet the real challenges of intercultural encounters: behavior management, speech accommodation, and role flexibility.

What is culture?

Myriads of definitions of culture abound, from the pragmatic ('the way we do things around here') to the academic ('a shared system of assumptions, values and beliefs of a people which result in characteristic behaviors').

But perhaps the best way to understand culture is by analogy with children learning their first language – instinctively, unconsciously, contingent upon their environment. They also are performing a feat of linguistic genius. Yet this is just one of many skills to be learnt: besides linguistic competence, children are also acquiring communicative competence, i.e. learning to use the appropriate speed and volume of speech, pitch and tone of voice, chuckles, sighs, gasps, etc. to communicate a highly nuanced range of emotions. Beyond these so-called paralinguistic features, children are also learning extra-linguistic communication: gestures, how and when to make eye contact, how close to stand to different people, when it is their turn to speak, etc.

As children continue to grow and to learn, they in time acquire cultural competence: a vast web of interconnected knowledge which includes, among other things, which groups of people should be accorded the most respect, which behaviors are acceptable for men and which for women, which foods one may eat, what is funny and what is not.[1] In short, children become fully socialized members of a community, and the constellation of values, norms and behaviors they have learned can be summed up with the word 'culture'.

Culture and communication

The culture we have acquired – the ways in which we have learned to see and think about the world – will of course influence how we communicate. By growing up in a certain society, we have come to expect certain behaviors (including verbal ones) as normal, others as appropriate only to specific situations, and others as taboo. We could say that our culture has fitted us with a set of filters that influence both our perceptions and our conceptions of the world.

In their book *Communicating with Strangers*, Gudykunst and Kim outline several notions about communication, including these assumptions:

- Communication is a process involving the encoding and decoding of messages.
- Communication takes place at varying levels of awareness.
- Communicators make predictions about the outcomes of their communication behavior.
- Intention is not a necessary condition for communication.
- Every communication message has a content dimension and a relationship dimension.[2]

The way we formulate our own ideas, and the way we interpret the utterances of others, are subject to various influences, whether your interlocutor be a human being from an exotic culture or the person most close to you ('Yes, dear, that's what I said, but that's not what I meant!').

The several layers of influence that surround each human being function as conceptual and perceptual filters, that is,

> mechanisms that delimit the number of alternatives from which we choose when we encode and decode messages. More specifically, the filters limit the predictions we make about how strangers might respond to our communication behavior. The nature of the predictions we make, in turn, influences the way we choose to encode our messages. Further, the filters delimit what stimuli we pay attention to and how we choose to interpret those stimuli when we decode incoming messages.[3]

Or put more plainly, our culture endows us with a set of expectations as to how people should act and react when we communicate with them. And these expectations are, at home and among our own, usually met. Once we are placed in an alien or a multicultural environment, however, we may find that our expectations are inaccurate; but this doesn't stop people from holding on to these expectations all the more tenaciously. This natural reaction is called ethnocentrism, the basic human tendency to believe that the way we learned to do certain things is the (only) right way.

Intercultural communication training

'Culture, a system of beliefs and values shared by a particular group of people,' writes Craig Storti,

> is an abstraction which can be appreciated intellectually, but it is behavior, the principal manifestation and most significant consequence of culture, that we actually experience. To put it another way: it is culture as encountered in behavior that we must learn to live with.
>
> The adjustments we must make to a new culture are invariably of two kinds: we have to adjust or get used to behavior on the part of the local people which annoys, confuses, or otherwise unsettles us; and we have to adjust our own behavior so that it does not annoy, confuse, or otherwise unsettle the local people. So long as we are put off by or consistently misconstrue the behavior of the locals and so long as we repeatedly provoke or baffle the locals by our own behavior, we can never expect to feel at ease abroad or to be wholly effective in our work.[4]

Aims and goals

The overall aim of the trainer is to raise the trainees' awareness of their own inherent ethnocentrism, and then offer exercises and experiences to help them leave that ethnocentrism behind.[5] Pragmatically, this means teaching people to manage their behavior so that it harmonizes with that of a different culture. But because behavior is the outward manifestation of a system of assumptions, values and beliefs, the trainee will also need to understand this system (appreciate it intellectually) and to feel comfortable living under it (accept it on an emotional, or affective, level).

Intercultural trainers have, therefore, three main *goals*. These are:

1 cognitive, that is, adding to the learner's stock of knowledge

2 affective, that is, changing the trainee's attitude by developing openness, tolerance, acceptance and awareness, and

3 behavioral, in which the trainee learns the 'dos and don'ts' of the new environment.[6]

Trainers also deliver *content*, the information to be conveyed:

• the 'what' of facts and figures, anecdotes and descriptions

• the 'how' of appropriate behavior in particular situations, rules of address and conduct, 'dos and don'ts', and

• the 'why' of cultural phenomena, using knowledge of the particular historical development of the target culture.

Finally, trainers must consider the *process* by which changes are effected in the trainee. A cognitive approach may be chosen, using such methods as lectures, readings and discussions. A more experiential approach is also possible, in which the trainee's temperament, emotions and interpersonal skills are brought into play. Examples of methods here include games, role-plays, simulations and ethnographic interviews.

The Intercultural Resource Pack offers trainers a wide range of materials with which to deliver the content of intercultural communication training. The activities help the trainer achieve the cognitive, affective and behavioral goals of training, and they serve as a springboard into the real world of experiential intercultural interaction. Through them the student should begin the enriching process of making the strange seem familiar and the dangerous seem delightful, and should gain that cultural understanding that grants us the sense and sensitivity to be both gracious hosts and gracious guests upon this island Earth.

Notes

1 Cf. Edward T. Hall's *The Silent Language*, New York: Anchor Books, 1997, particularly chapter 3, 'The Vocabulary of Culture'.

2 Gudykunst, W. and Kim, Y., *Communicating with Strangers: An Approach to Intercultural Communications* (4th Edition), New York: McGraw-Hill, 2002, pp. 6–9.

3 Ibid., p. 31.

4 Craig Storti, *The Art of Crossing Cultures* (2nd Edition), Yarmouth: Intercultural Press, 2001, p. 15.

5 Cf. Milton J. Bennett, 'A developmental approach to training for intercultural sensitivity', *International Journal of Intercultural Relations*, Vol. 10, 1986, pp. 179–200.

6 Cf. Janet M. Bennett, 'Modes of cross-cultural training: Conceptualizing cross-cultural training as education', *International Journal of Intercultural Relations*, Vol. 10, 1986, pp. 117–134, and Virginia Milhouse, 'Intercultural Communication Education and Training Goals, Content, and Method', *International Journal of Intercultural Relations*, Vol. 29, No. 1, 1996, pp. 69–95.

Recommended reading

Acton, William R. and Walker de Felix, Judith (1986) 'Acculturation and mind' in Valdez, Joyce Merrill (ed.) *Culture Bound: Bridging the Cultural Gap in Language Teaching*, pp. 20–32, New York: Cambridge University Press.

Brislin, R. W. (1999) *Understanding Culture's Influence on Behavior* (2nd Edition), Fort Worth: Harcourt Brace Jovanovich.

Brislin, R. and Cushner, K. (1996) *Intercultural Interactions: A Practical Guide* (2nd Edition), Newbury Park, CA: Sage.

Fantini, Alvino (1997) *New Ways of Teaching Culture*, Alexandria: TESOL.

Gibson, R. (2002) *Intercultural Business Communication*, Oxford: Oxford University Press.

Gudykunst, W. and Kim, Y. (2002) *Communicating with Strangers: An Approach to Intercultural Communications* (4th Edition), New York: McGraw-Hill.

Hall, Edward T. (1997) *Beyond Culture*, New York: Anchor Books.

Hall, Edward T. (1997) *The Silent Language*, New York: Anchor Books.

Hall, Edward T. (1997) and Hall, Mildred Reed (1989) *Understanding Cultural Differences: Germans, French and Americans*, Yarmouth: Intercultural Press.

Hofstede, G. and Hofstede, G.J. (2004) *Cultures and Organizations*: *Software of the Mind* (Third Millennium Edition), New York: McGraw-Hill.

International Journal of Intercultural Relations, published quarterly since 1977 by Elsevier Science Ltd, ISSN 0147-1767 (see especially Vol. 10, 1986).

Landis, D. and Bhagat, R. S. (eds.) (1996) *Handbook of Intercultural Training* (2nd Edition), Thousand Oaks: Sage Publications.

Samovar, L. A. and Porter, R. E. (2003) *Intercultural Communication: A Reader* (10th Edition), New York: Wadsworth.

Storti, Craig (2001) *The Art of Crossing Cultures* (2nd Edition), Yarmouth: Intercultural Press.

Trompenaars, Alfons, Hampden-Turner, Charles and Trompenaars, Fons (1997) *Riding the Waves of Culture: Understanding Diversity in Global Business*, New York: McGraw-Hill.

Language reference

Some of these phrases may be useful for groups of students when discussing the activities.

Asking for and giving opinions	Do you think that …? I think … I feel that … is important.
Agreeing and disagreeing	I agree with you (up to a point). I'm afraid I don't agree. That may be true, but … Yes, but on the other hand …
Making suggestions	Should we include this? What about including this? I think we should include this. Would it be a good idea to …? Could we also say that …? Maybe it's important to … Don't you think …?
Checking	So you mean that …? Do you mean to say that …? What exactly do you mean by …? Was that eight or eighty?
Summarising	To summarise, then … To sum up, then, … Let's just summarise the position.
Comparatives and superlatives	This is more important than … … is of less value than … … isn't as useful as … … is the most important thing. These are the least useful.
Discussing a hypothetical situation	I'd want to know … Wouldn't you need to know about …? It would be useful to know if … I think I'd want information about … Would … be useful?
Likelihood	I'm (absolutely) sure/certain this will increase. This is (quite) likely to increase. This may/might increase. It is (highly/very) unlikely this will increase. This (definitely/certainly) won't increase.
Conditions	If we choose this, we will have problems. If we included both items, there would be too many. If we had known that, we would have acted differently. If I were in their position, I would …
Obligation	We really must do this. It's essential we do this. It's important we do this. We should do the following …
Sequencing	First we should …, then we should …, and finally we should …
Explaining	This is a good idea because … That's why I said that.
Coming in	Can I come in here? Can I just say something?
Asking and challenging	Are we sure this is true? Do you (really) think this is important?
Fillers and refiners	Actually, … As a matter of fact, … Basically, …

Teacher's notes and activities

1.1 Brainstorming: What is culture for you?

Aims
• To collect as many ideas as possible on the many different components of culture.
• To show how the concept of culture, and its components, can be interpreted differently by different individuals or groups.

Procedure

1 If your students are not familiar with mind maps, spend a few minutes developing a simple mind map on the board or overhead projector. Choose a subject you know well, based on the mind map in this activity. For example:

   Central topic: media; branching topics: television, radio, newspapers, magazines. Extend if necessary (for example, newspapers can be morning or evening, national or local). Make sure they understand that the idea of a mind map is to loosely link together different ideas and thoughts around a central theme.

   Introduce the concept of culture by asking questions like:

   • What is culture for you?
   • What does it involve?
   • What shapes culture?

   Invite the students to express their ideas as freely as possible, without too much discussion at this stage.

2 Ask the students to look at the mind map, and check that the words are understood and the links clear. Explain that the elements given are not intended to be a complete list, but simply a selection. If necessary, go through a branch such as 'Social life', showing the links through to the final column. Ask individuals for examples of how such aspects as 'gender' (the differing social and work roles of male and female) are viewed in their own cultures.

3 Form pairs or groups to do task 1: find suitable words to fit in the spaces numbered 1 to 6. The words should be relatively easy to find, but allow time for discussion, and accept anything which students can explain satisfactorily. Compare and discuss results.

4 Do the same for task 2, either in groups as before, or in an open session, asking for ideas on ways of continuing some of the lines outwards. For example, the line Physical – body language – gestures could be continued with 'hands, body, feet', with students then giving examples of how gestures can differ from culture to culture.

Outcomes

Suggestions for the missing words are:

1 traffic   2 independence   3 spoken
4 work times   5 home   6 speed

Development

Continuation of the lines could be extensively developed by students who are particularly interested. Some may wish to restructure and add new elements to the mind map as well as extend it.

Many of the topics can lead to discussion of emotive or abstract topics such as driving habits ('traffic'), fashion ('dress'), bluntness ('directness of speech').

Discussion could also centre around the origin of the word 'culture'. It is based on the Latin word 'cultus', meaning growing or cultivating a crop or a plant. This illustrates one important aspect of culture, which is that it is something which has always and will always be changing and modifying itself in both large and small ways.

Encourage students to be open in their definition of culture. It is a very flexible concept, and they should be encouraged to be open and tolerant.

Although this mind map attempts to divide up culture into different parts, students will realise that there is a large amount of overlap, because of the complexity of the subject.

To begin with, students may suggest some obvious differences between cultures such as food, dress and language. Acknowledge that these are indeed differences, at the same time encouraging them to bring out less easily perceived differences such as attitudes to authority or family.

Linked activities

1.2, 1.3

Further reading

For examples of dividing up culture into seen and unseen, implicit and explicit, etc., see chapter 2 ('What is Culture?') of

The Silent Language, by E. T. Hall, 1997, New York: Anchor Books

as well as chapter 4 ('Hidden Culture') of the book

Beyond Culture, by E.T. Hall, 1997, New York: Anchor Books.

1.1   Brainstorming: What is culture for you?

What is 'culture' for you? The word has many meanings and is open to many interpretations.

The aim of this mind map is to try to identify as many of the components of culture as possible. Follow the lines out from the central word 'culture'.

1 Complete the spaces numbered 1 to 6 with a suitable word or phrase.

2 Continue the lines outwards with suitable ideas.

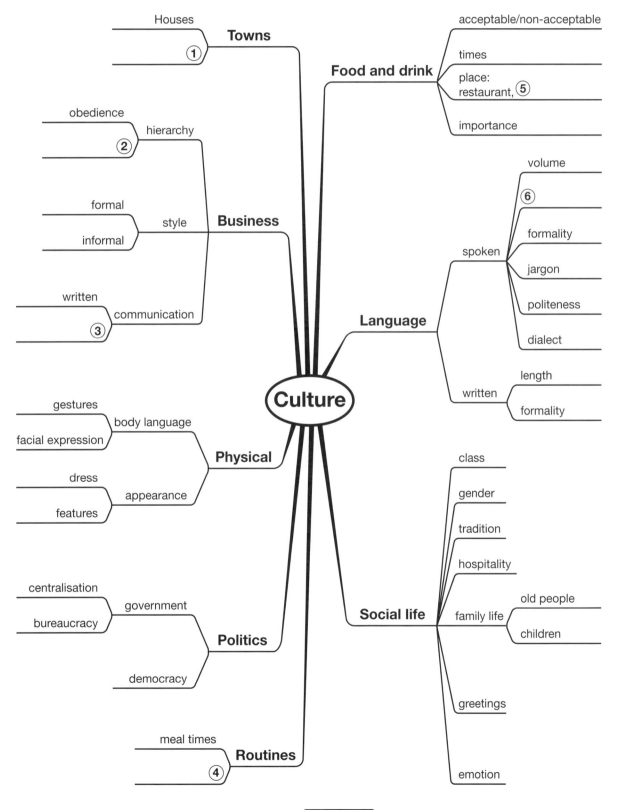

Aims

- To explore the concept of culture.
- To develop ideas about the main components of culture.

This activity may be used as a shorter alternative to **1.1**, or as an addition to it.

Procedure

1 Ask the students if they can give a short definition of what culture is for them.

2 Read the introduction to the activity, to raise awareness of the factors listed in the three bullet points. Culture:

- can be influenced by many factors such as geography, history and climate
- can be shared not only by the members of a national culture such as the Japanese or the Brazilians, but also by people of one company, one region or one profession
- can show itself in observable behaviour such as gestures, but also in non-observable phenomena such as attitudes and taboos.

3 Ask the students to look at the five definitions of culture. Check any unknown vocabulary and that they understand the ideas.

4 Working in pairs or small groups, students should work through tasks 1 to 3. Encourage them to use as a basis for discussion the three bulleted points at the beginning of the activity. Each of the definitions carries expressions relevant to these points, such as:

- 'conditioned', 'programming' 'learned programmes', 'passed on'
- 'group of people', 'you', 'the human mind', 'generation', 'a society'
- 'beliefs, values and norms', 'think, feel, interpret and react', 'action', 'know and believe'.

5 Ask volunteers from each pair or group to present and comment on their group's choice with any comments, additions or even internal disagreements.

6 Encourage comparison and discussion of the different definitions. This should lead to a more open discussion of the concept and components of culture.

Outcomes

A search for their 'best' definition may be motivating, but the most important thing in this activity is to generate, compare and expand ideas. It will be useful to point out that each of the different definitions focuses on different features:

A abstract ideas such as beliefs and knowledge as well as the idea of a collective group
B reactions, conditioning and programming
C conditioning and programming
D actions, conditioning and programming
E abstract ideas such as beliefs and knowledge as well as society.

Development

Finding the 'perfect' definition will be difficult if not impossible. Use the definitions to help students become more aware of how cultures develop and how they manifest themselves. If the three concepts shown in the bullet points can be made clear, they will form a good basis for further understanding.

Linked activities

1.1, 1.3

Further reading

A thoroughgoing exercise in the definition of culture was undertaken in

Culture: A Critical Review of Concepts and Definitions, by A.L. Kroeber, C. Kluckholm and W. Untereiner, 2001, New York: Greenwood Press.

For a more concise discussion with an emphasis on culture's inherent values, see chapter 1 ('Values and Culture') of

Culture's Consequences: Comparing values, behaviors, institutions and organizations across nations, by Geert Hofstede, 2001 2nd Edition, Thousand Oaks, CA: Sage Publications.

1.2 Defining the word 'culture'

'Culture' can mean different things to different people.

Think about:

- how culture is created – by geography, climate, history, coincidence?
- what groups of people can be said to have a culture – races, countries, companies?
- in what ways you see, hear or experience it – by behaviour, attitudes, gestures?

Look at these five definitions of culture.

1 Select the one you think is closest to your own idea.
2 Identify any missing elements in each definition.
3 If not satisfied, produce your own, better definition.

A

The sum total of all the beliefs, values and norms shared by a group of people.

B

The way you have been conditioned in a society to think, feel, interpret and react.

C

The collective programming of the human mind.

D

A large pool of experience composed of learned programmes for action and passed on from generation to generation.

E

All you need to know and believe in order to be accepted in a society.

My definition:

1.3 | The culture iceberg

Aims

- To explore how features of cultures range from the easily recognisable to the almost imperceptible.
- To develop an awareness of this range.

Procedure

1 Ask students what they know about icebergs in order to elicit the fact that a large part (about seven eighths) is normally below water level. They may observe similar characteristics in, for example, people (some have well-hidden characteristics) or families.

2 Check that students understand the significance of the illustration and then present task 1, which deals with national culture in general, rather than one specific culture. Ask them to put each of the components from the list into one of the categories A, B and C. They should work in pairs or small groups to complete the task.

3 Take each section – A, B and C – separately, asking a spokesperson from each group to run through their list, and ask for comparisons and comments from other groups.

4 Now do task 2, which relates this topic to a specific culture. Form groups to examine one particular culture (the members may be from that culture or not, but should have some experience of it). They should list at least two components from each category which are important in that culture.

5 Ask a spokesperson from each group to briefly summarise what the group has discussed. Invite comment and discussion.

6 Brainstorm task 3, which will collect any elements identified in the discussions which do not appear in the list.

Outcomes

The categorisation of components should produce a certain amount of agreement, with plenty of scope for differing interpretations and consequent discussion.

This is one possible categorisation:

A artefacts, directness of speech in business, driving habits, greetings, emotion shown in public, physical gestures

B balance between work and home, corruption, family life, gender – roles of males and females, humour, organisation of companies, personal friendship, press and other media, punctuality in business, social life: public and private

C democracy, social organisation and class, treatment of outsiders/foreigners, values and beliefs.

Development

Tasks 2 and 3 give students the opportunity to think about the characteristics of different national cultures. This could lead to work on profiling different cultures (see Linked activities below).

They could also give rise to thinking about the difference between profiling your own culture as opposed to profiling cultures to which you do not belong, for which the Linked activities below will also be a useful follow-up.

Linked activities

1.4, 1.5, 3.3, 3.4

Further reading

Other models which help to visualise culture include Hofstede's pyramid, see pp. 14–17 in

Culture's Consequences: Comparing values, behaviors, institutions and organizations across nations, by Geert Hofstede, 2001 2nd Edition, Thousand Oaks, CA: Sage Publications

and the onion diagram in

Culturally Speaking: Managing Rapport in Talk Across Cultures, by Helen Spenser-Oatey, 2001, New York: Continuum International Publishing Group.

1.3 The culture iceberg

When you observe people from a certain culture, some characteristics – such as dress and the way people greet each other – are easy to see. Others are not so easy.

Culture is sometimes compared to an iceberg, some of which is visible, but much of which is difficult to see, or invisible.

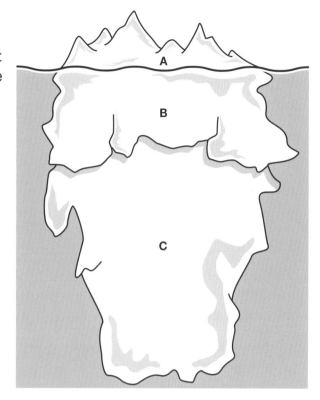

1 Look at the list of components of national culture, and place each one in one of the three categories:

A things which you can recognise quite easily

B things which take some time to recognise

C things which you recognise only when you are very familiar with a culture.

Artefacts: art and architecture	☐	Humour	☐
Balance between work and home	☐	Organisation of companies	☐
Corruption	☐	Personal friendship	☐
Democracy	☐	Physical gestures	☐
Directness of speech in business	☐	Press and other media	☐
Driving habits	☐	Punctuality in business	☐
Emotion shown in public	☐	Social life: public and private	☐
Family life	☐	Social organisation and class	☐
Gender – roles of males and females	☐	Treatment of outsiders/foreigners	☐
Greetings	☐	Values and beliefs	☐

2 Are any of these more important than others in understanding a particular national culture with which you are familiar?

3 Add any other elements which you think are important in defining a national culture you know.

1.4 | Cultural briefing

Aims
- To examine the usefulness of cultural briefing for people going to live, work or holiday abroad.
- To identify the most important elements in cultural briefing.

Procedure

1 Check students' understanding of the term 'cultural briefing'. If necessary, explain that it consists of finding out about a culture or country you are about to visit or have contact with. Ask for examples of when it might be necessary, such as a first business trip to China or Peru. Ask the students for some elements which they think would be included in a cultural briefing. Discuss these points briefly in pairs or small groups and compare results.

2 Present task 1 and briefly check that students understand the words in the list and what they have to do: at this point they are not expected to know the information, simply to think what it would be most useful for them to know, based on their previous conceptions of the target culture. Working in pairs or groups, students select the six most useful things they would like to know. For example, Western students with little knowledge of China may feel that the sheer size of the country will make regional differences important, or that the 'inscrutability' of the Chinese may make silence a useful attribute in some situations.
Ask a spokesperson from each group to present the results, allowing time for comment and discussion.

3 Present task 2. This time the target culture should be to some degree familiar, so the exercise should be similar to the previous one, but slightly quicker and easier. Students could work individually. Compare results, asking for explanations of why certain points were chosen. (For example, in culture X, visitors should be aware that pre-planning for meetings is very important.) Present and compare results.

4 Present task 3, which may be done for homework. The presentation, by an individual or a group, should take the form of a cultural briefing as described above. If it is written, photocopy the students' work and distribute it to the others.

Outcomes

There is no 'correct' selection of components from the list, as it will depend on individual experience and taste. But make students aware of the fact that some items are practical, such as tipping in restaurants, while others are more abstract, such as respect for authority. Usually the former are easier to identify than the latter. It may be interesting to ask students to compare the balance between the two in the different selections.

Development

Cultural briefing is available in many types of book and document (see Further reading below), and on a growing number of websites. It has an important role in preparing people to cope with living in a new cultural environment. Encourage students to explore this area as much as they wish. However, make them aware that cultural briefing, without direct experience, may also encourage the formation of stereotypical views. Encourage them always to be cautious about views unconfirmed by their own experience.

Linked activities

1.5, 2.5, 2.7, 3.3, 3.4

Further reading

For the cross-cultural trainer it is always important to match the method of training to the kind and amount of information to be covered. For a useful discussion of the difference between briefing, orientation, training and education, see pp. 117–34 ('Modes of cross-cultural training: Conceptualizing cross-cultural training as education') in
International Journal of Intercultural Relations, Vol. 10, by Janet M. Bennett, 1986
and pp. 69–95, 'Intercultural Communication Education and Training Goals, Content and Method', in
International Journal of Intercultural Relations, Vol. 29, No. 1, by Virginia Milhouse, 1996.

Cultural briefing

Cultural briefing is the process of finding out about another culture, especially in preparation for a period of residence, a business trip or a holiday.

Some types of information can be learnt about beforehand, such as the organisation of the public transport system, and forms of address (Doctor, Mr, etc.), but it may be better to discover others through direct experience.

Look at the list below.

1 Choose a country whose culture you know little about, and from the list pick out the six things you would find it most useful to know before you visited the country on a business trip.

2 Choose a country whose culture you are familiar with, and do the same.

3 Prepare a short introduction (spoken or written) which would be useful for people about to make a business trip to that country.

Attitudes to alcohol	Political system
Attitudes to foreigners	Preparation for meetings
Dealing with emergencies	Public transport
Demography – population spread	Regions
Formality of dress in business	Religion and its importance
Geography	Respect for authority
History	Shop opening times
Hospitality	Silence – its acceptability in conversation and meetings
Housing standards	Thinking – analytical or intuitive?
Local products	Tipping in restaurants
Meal times	Titles – Mrs, Dr, etc., and their equivalents
Money – paying restaurant bills	
Physical distance between people when they speak	

1.5 | Cultural briefing: The Swedes

Aims
To present the idea of cultural briefing and to evaluate its usefulness.

Procedure

1 If your students are not from Sweden, introduce this activity by asking them what they know about Sweden.

   - Where is Sweden?
   - What's the landscape like?
   - What about the weather?
   - What do you know about the people?
   - What do you know about Swedish culture?

   If students are from Sweden, ask them what they think people from other cultures know about Sweden and the Swedes.

2 Ask students to read the introduction and task 1. Check that they understand the sentences in the list and what they have to do. Make sure they understand that at this stage they are not being asked to discuss the relative truth of the statements, but simply to choose the six most useful ones for the visitor. It is not necessary to put the six things of most value in order of importance.

3 Working individually or in small groups, students should prepare their lists.

   Each group should prepare their list on paper, whiteboard, flipchart or OHP transparency. Compare results and ask for justification of each choice.

4 If the class contains students with experience or knowledge of Swedish culture, move on to task 2. Invite them to give their views on the validity of the statements, and on how the information they contain can help guide the visitor in everyday life and business. Students do not necessarily have to agree with the statements (those referring to humour and the 'Swedish model' may easily be challenged), but discussion of the issues they raise should be seen as a useful awareness-raising exercise.

Outcomes

This activity should draw out the distinction between geographical and political facts on the one hand, and more subjective areas such as moral or social values on the other. It should show that it can be relatively easy to explain and discuss the former objectively, but the latter require more careful thought.

Suggestions for the two main categories of information:

More objective/practical: 1, 2, 3, 7, 13
More subjective: 4, 5, 6, 8, 9, 10, 11, 12, 14, 15, 16

The activity should highlight the different degrees of importance attached by students to different types of information. This in turn should show how cultural briefing needs to cover a wide range of topics in order to meet a wide variety of needs.

Development

You may decide to extend this exercise to your students' own cultures. Ask them to create a list for people visiting their countries. Compare lists and see if many common features emerge, such as a majority of practical tips, revealing a pragmatic approach; or subjective ones, showing a more interpretive attitude. Raise the question:

Does the choice reflect on the culture itself, or more on the student choosing the topics?

Linked activities

1.4, 2.5, 2.7, 3.4

Further reading

Culture also influences our judgements as to which and what kind of information is important in any given situation. See

Perception and Identity in Intercultural Communication, by Marshall R. Singer, 1998, Yarmouth: Intercultural Press.

For excellent monographs on various cultures, visit the website of the Intercultural Press at http://interculturalpress.com

1.5 | Cultural briefing: The Swedes

Look at the following information prepared for someone who is about to go on a business trip to Sweden, and who has little previous experience of the culture or the country.

1 Choose from the list below the six things you think they would find most useful, and the six least useful.

1 Sweden has almost nine million inhabitants with a low population density (about nine million people in about 450,000 square kilometres).

2 It is a kingdom with a constitutional monarch.

3 The prime minister and the cabinet are responsible to Parliament.

4 The 'Swedish model' or 'middle way' represents a mixture of caring socialism with individual capitalist entrepreneurialism.

5 Differences in income are less marked than in many other countries.

6 People tend to be shy, reserved and not very talkative.

7 Public and private sector services such as transport and restaurants tend to work efficiently.

8 Swedes tend to speak English well, and to be well travelled.

9 At school they learn to think logically and to behave in a restrained manner.

10 Teamwork is common and appreciated.

11 Gestures and physical contact are not generally approved of.

12 Swedes usually plan appointments well in advance.

13 Holidays are usually taken between late June and early August.

14 People feel attached to their local region.

15 Humour is less important than in some other cultures.

16 Sensitive subjects such as sex or religion are often avoided in conversation.

2 If you know something about the Swedes, say whether you think the statements are valid or not.

Aims

- To consider the differences between the conflicting forces of global production and distribution on the one hand, and strong local marketing on the other.
- To show the impact of these forces on business cultures.

This activity may be more demanding than others, given its political dimensions, but it is accessible to younger students through their familiarity with multinational companies which target younger people, like McDonalds and Nokia.

Procedure

1 Begin by discussing the word 'globe' with the class. If you have a globe, use it as an aid to get this discussion started. Ask students for any expressions they know which use 'globe' or 'global' and for their meanings (see Outcomes).

2 Check that students understand the words used. Ask them to clarify the two main elements mentioned at the beginning – one based on logistics and material things, the other on marketing and people.

3 Introduce task 1. The three statements highlight the contrast between:

- the ever increasing global scale of world commerce, and
- the reaction against it – the commercial need to recognise the differences between local markets, and the reaction of people to what they consider to be the monolithic nature of multinational companies.

Ask students to work in small groups to study the statements and agree on a group response, if possible. Ask a spokesperson from one group to tell the class what they have decided, and invite others in the class to comment and discuss.

4 Introduce task 2 with a short discussion of the forces referred to in **a** and **b**. For example:

a McDonalds, Nike, Nokia and Coca-Cola, who through their branding encourage local people to accept a product and therefore a lifestyle which will owe more to its origins (often, but not always, American) than to local preference.

b the increase in local representation, growth of local craft work, the encouragement of minority languages and local dialects, and the popularity of local clubs and organisations for activities such as traditional dancing, local history and folklore.

5 Ask students to work in their small groups again for a few minutes and then return to a whole class discussion. Draw up a list on the board or overhead projector, and use it to speculate about the world in 20 years' time or more.

Outcomes

Terms mentioned in Procedure 1 may include:

global competition
global corporation
global demand
global economy
global market
global marketing
global view
global village
global warming
globalisation
glocalisation
go global
operate globally

Development

For students particularly interested in this subject, further discussion could be encouraged by highlighting its paradox.

To minimise costs, large companies need standardised production methods and uniform products, and to achieve large sales they need as big a market as possible. But they also need to appeal to a wide variety of different markets. You can raise the question of 'branding', whereby certain products (e.g. Pepsi-Cola and Adidas) are made to be instantly recognisable, and so can be sold in the same form worldwide. Global branding is bad for local cultures, although marketing strategies often have to allow for local variations.

Other issues which could interest students are:

- sport sponsorship by multinationals
- worldwide sports tournaments.

Linked activities

1.7, 1.10, 4.8, 4.9

Further reading

For a discussion on global strategy and culture, see pp. 3–14 in

International Dimensions of Organizational Behavior, by Nancy Adler, 2001, Cincinnati: South-Western College Publishing.

One way out of the dilemma of standardised production versus multiple markets has been offered in

Mass Customization: The New Frontier in Business Competition, by Joseph Pine, 1999, Harvard Business School Press.

1.6 | The global dimension

One of the biggest challenges facing multinational companies in the 21st century is to 'think global, act local' – how to be on the one hand:

- a global supplier of quality goods and services using a closely coordinated supply chain and organisation

and, on the other

- a local company whose people speak the customer's language.

It is claimed that the first of these phenomena – the global organisation – is destroying local cultures by imposing one standard way of buying, thinking and acting. Or, at least, that cultures are becoming more similar to each other.

What do you think?

1 For each of the following statements on this subject, show how much you agree or disagree by putting the appropriate number in the box:
5 = Agree strongly   4 = Agree   3 = No opinion   2 = Disagree   1 = Disagree strongly
Compare and discuss your results.

> **1** The further the world shrinks, the greater the need for cultures to be different. ☐

> **2** Modern civilisation requires that all human societies will become increasingly similar. ☐

> **3** As economies get closer, cultures get further apart. ☐

2 Give examples of how national cultures are:
a becoming more and more like each other, for example, through the effects of worldwide publicity, franchises and sponsorships on the way people dress, eat and behave
b asserting their own identities, for example, in the way people speak, the traditional goods they produce and the local organisations they form.

Aims

- To examine the changes that have taken place in the world economy and society in the recent past.
- To explore the impact this has had on national cultures and on behaviour.

Procedure

1 Introduce the idea of how, for many people, contact with other nationalities and cultures has increased because of easier international travel and communication. Ask for examples, such as better telecommunications, satellite TV, the internet, cheaper and more frequent flights, more tourist facilities, and increased educational exchanges. Ask for ideas as to how this might change people's attitudes as well as their behaviour. Travel broadens the mind – or does it?

2 Introduce task 1. Ask students to read through the statements and make sure the meaning is clear. Most of them refer to the world of business, but there are also references to education (3), customer service (9), politics (12) and society in general (15). Form pairs or small groups and ask them to read and respond to the statements, trying to produce one set of answers for the group, but allowing individual differences if preferred.

3 Ask a spokesperson from each group to report back the results. Either ask each group to illustrate the results on the whiteboard, and then compare; or go through each statement one by one, comparing each group's results. Encourage discussion.

4 Introduce task 2. Each group should draw up a list after a brief discussion. Changes may have been observed in the students' own lifetime, or they may have heard parents or elderly people comparing life in their youth with life today. Try to bring in examples both from the world of work and from society in general.

Outcomes

In task 1, a wide range of opinions could be expressed by students, and discussion should be encouraged. Items like numbers 5 and 6 may be difficult to challenge, but some, like 4, 7, 8, 14 and 15, are more contentious.

In task 2, responses will vary from group to group, but encourage the comparison in attitudes (more informed, broad-minded, tolerant?) as well as appearance and behaviour (smarter, more informal, better communicators?).

Development

Students should be encouraged to challenge simplified views of 'glocalisation' (global activities with local marketing presence) and 'globalphobia' – the idea that individual cultures are all being swallowed up by one global culture. Also raise the question of whether increased contact between cultures actually leads to easier and better relations. Get students to give examples.

Focus on the implications of some of the phenomena mentioned here, and the effects on everyday life. This could lead to a discussion of which developments have been for the better and which for the worse.

Linked activities

1.6, 1.9, 1.10, 4.8

Further reading

The effects of globalisation on culture (and vice versa) are discussed in pp. 35–51, 'Communication in a Global Village', by Dean Barnlund, in

Basic Concepts of Intercultural Communication: Selected Readings, edited by Milton J. Bennett, 1998, Yarmouth: Intercultural Press.

Technical, commercial and political developments over the last few years have affected society in general, and business in particular.

1 Look at the following statements which compare the state of business today with that of 25 years ago.

  a Put the appropriate number in the box:
  1 = True   2 = False   3 = Don't know

  b For those that you think are true, explain how they affect and change people's attitudes and behaviour.

Compared with 25 years ago ...

1 Manufacturing companies source their materials from a wider range of suppliers. ☐

2 Branding of products is done more on a worldwide scale. ☐

3 Educational exchanges give people more experience of living in other countries. ☐

4 Small companies have less hope of surviving. ☐

5 Improved telecommunications have made life easier for most companies. ☐

6 Travel is easier and more accepted by business people. ☐

7 Computers have led to higher standards of performance at work. ☐

8 Company organisation has become simpler. ☐

9 Customers expect to be treated more on their own terms. ☐

10 Employees of large companies must expect to change their place of work more regularly. ☐

11 Lifelong employment with one company is less likely. ☐

12 Political barriers between east and west are less strong. ☐

13 Projects require people to work more harmoniously together. ☐

14 Large companies resemble each other more and more. ☐

15 Business people understand other cultures better. ☐

---

2 Explain briefly the four things that have changed most in your own national culture in the last 25 years or so.

Aims

- To examine the expectations people have when meeting people from other cultures.
- To see how these expectations can affect the attitudes and behaviour of both sides.

Procedure

1   Ask the students to imagine that they are about to meet a person they have never seen before – a surprise visitor or a long-lost relative, for example, or a person they have often heard spoken of but never met. What expectations would they have, and what would they be based on? Also ask the students what they expected to see and experience when moving to a new school or a new company. What were their expectations of their future colleagues? Do we all form the same picture?

   Draw out the fact that these ideas are usually very subjective, sometimes based on false information or emotion. Draw the parallel with our expectations of people from other cultures: our ideas of them are often based on scanty information or experience, but often affect the way we behave towards them.

2   Ask students to read task 1, and check that they understand the words and the task: they should select two different nationalities with which they are familiar and try to predict what preconceived ideas each of the two characters will have about the other. At this stage do not raise the question of where these ideas come from. Form pairs or groups to do the task, and ask a spokesperson to report back. Discuss and compare results.

3   Introduce task 2, which is simply a discussion of the usefulness or otherwise of expectations. Though they are a useful and natural way of preparing for an unknown situation, they carry the possible dangers of inaccuracy, prejudice and stereotyping. Some examples of both useful and potentially harmful expectations may well have come out in the preceding discussions.

Outcomes

Task 1 will not yield uniform results, but should illustrate the point made in task 2 that expectations can have both positive and negative effects.

Development

The discussions above should lead to a consideration of what we think about other nationalities and other cultures before we actually come into contact with them. It should raise the question of prejudice and stereotypes. Everybody makes assumptions about people or situations with which they are not familiar. These assumptions are a necessary part of preparation, and can contribute to a successful contact. They can also lead to the creation of stereotypes and prejudices which are forced onto the situation, and which may clash with the reality. A person who sees ready-formed attitudes in another may well find them offensive, particularly if, as can often be the case with stereotypes, those views are negative.

Linked activities

1.4, 1.5, 2.5, 2.8, 6.4

Further reading

The crucial role that expectations play in our experience of other cultures is explained in

The Art of Crossing Cultures (2nd Edition), by Craig Storti, 2001, Yarmouth: Intercultural Press.

See also:

Understanding Culture's Influence on Behavior, by Richard Brislin, 1999, Fort Worth: Harcourt Brace Jovanovich.

1.8 Expectations

Before meeting someone from another culture, people often form ideas of what to expect. These may be founded on fact, on hearsay or on imagination.

These expectations could be a useful form of preparation, or they could lead to stereotyped ideas which get in the way of successful communication.

1 Think of two different nationalities. Imagine what qualities people from each of those countries would expect to find in the other before they met. Choose from the list below, but add any others you think likely.

communication in short sentences	little direct eye contact
direct style of communication	lots of talk about food
displays of emotion	lots of gesticulation
emotional volatility	loud speech
emphasis on entertainment	periods of silence
extrovert behaviour	quiet speech
extreme politeness	reserved behaviour
rapid speech	slowness to speak
indirect style of communication	talkativeness
limited body language	

2 Do you think that expectations that you have before you meet someone from a different culture are generally helpful or unhelpful?

1.9 | Case study: One person's experience

Aims
- To examine an example of a situation in which two different cultures have to work together.
- To think about how to make such a situation work.

Procedure

1 Ideally, students should read the case study before coming to the lesson. Explain the aim of this activity, which is based on a real business case.

2 Check that students understand the text and the list of possible actions. In task 1, it is worth noting that the suggestions fall into two broad categories: steps to modify Dave's behaviour, and steps to modify that of the local company.

3 Divide the class into pairs or small groups and ask them to discuss the pros and cons of each of the possible actions listed, prioritise them and make any additions they feel necessary. Each group should appoint one person to take brief notes.

4 Ask the spokesperson from each group to present their group's ideas by summarising the main points. Allow time for questions and comments.

5 Encourage comparisons and discussion of each group's ideas.

Outcomes

It should be possible for students to arrive at a realistic list of actions which should include opportunities for development for both the Canadian and the Taiwanese groups. It might be stressful for everybody involved in the project to include all the options.

Discussion of possible actions that Dave could take should lead to an awareness of the way in which normal business management problems can become more complicated where there is a strong cultural element – in this case the clear contrast between Canadian and Taiwanese styles. This activity also provides scope for experiencing a real decision-making situation.

Development

Students should work in the same groups to prepare a short action plan for Dave and his company. The form and length of the report should be adapted to the experience of the group. Each group should prepare its action plan on paper, whiteboard, flipchart, or OHP transparency. Written reports can be distributed between the groups for comparison.

Linked activities

1.7, 1.10, 6.11

Further reading

For further exercises and case studies see

Intercultural Business Communication, by Robert Gibson, 2002, Oxford: Oxford University Press

and also pp. 207–214, 'Case Study: Salman Rushdie and The Satanic Verses', by Janet M. Bennett in

Intercultural Sourcebook: Cross-Cultural Training Methods (Volume 1), by Sandra M. Fowler and Monica G. Mumford, 1995, Yarmouth: Intercultural Press.

1.9 Case study: One person's experience

This case study exemplifies a contrast between two working cultures: Canadian and Taiwanese.

Canada

Taiwan

Read the text and the list of possible actions. Then make recommendations as to what the Canadian should do.

1 Choose from the list below those activities you think he should carry out.

2 Rank them in order of priority.

3 Add any other actions you think necessary.

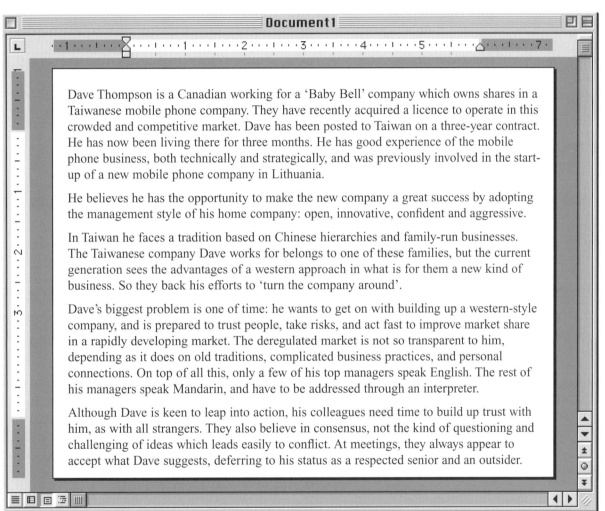

Document1

Dave Thompson is a Canadian working for a 'Baby Bell' company which owns shares in a Taiwanese mobile phone company. They have recently acquired a licence to operate in this crowded and competitive market. Dave has been posted to Taiwan on a three-year contract. He has now been living there for three months. He has good experience of the mobile phone business, both technically and strategically, and was previously involved in the start-up of a new mobile phone company in Lithuania.

He believes he has the opportunity to make the new company a great success by adopting the management style of his home company: open, innovative, confident and aggressive.

In Taiwan he faces a tradition based on Chinese hierarchies and family-run businesses. The Taiwanese company Dave works for belongs to one of these families, but the current generation sees the advantages of a western approach in what is for them a new kind of business. So they back his efforts to 'turn the company around'.

Dave's biggest problem is one of time: he wants to get on with building up a western-style company, and is prepared to trust people, take risks, and act fast to improve market share in a rapidly developing market. The deregulated market is not so transparent to him, depending as it does on old traditions, complicated business practices, and personal connections. On top of all this, only a few of his top managers speak English. The rest of his managers speak Mandarin, and have to be addressed through an interpreter.

Although Dave is keen to leap into action, his colleagues need time to build up trust with him, as with all strangers. They also believe in consensus, not the kind of questioning and challenging of ideas which leads easily to conflict. At meetings, they always appear to accept what Dave suggests, deferring to his status as a respected senior and an outsider.

Dave decides he must do something. He draws up the following list of possible actions:

- learn Mandarin
- bring in more Western managers
- organise lectures for his employees on Western business practices
- learn more about Taiwan
- slow down his approach
- send some of his managers to work in North America
- organise a one-day seminar on business cultures
- organise a meeting at which all the cultural problems are discussed
- bring in a local management consultant

Aims
- To show how companies need both a global and a local approach to business.
- To analyse measures helping a company to meet the challenges of global business.

Procedure

1 Students could read the case study and fill in the boxes before coming to the lesson. Check that students understand the words and what they have to do.

2 Form pairs or small groups to fill in or check the contents of the boxes.

  Ask a spokesperson from one group to read out their replies, and invite comments and discussion.

3 With an experienced group, ask students to look at task 2, spending as much time as their experience allows on prioritising and adding to the list. The results could be summarised in a short presentation.

Outcomes

Some of the actions contain elements of both objectives, but a possible classification is:

1 A **2** B **3** A **4** A **5** B **6** B **7** A **8** A **9** B
10 B **11** B **12** B

But disagreement is likely and will fuel discussion.

Development

Where students have considerable experience of international business, it could be useful to compare the relative value of practical issues, such as cheap sourcing and efficient production and logistics, with the more long-term issues of investing time and resources in developing positive attitudes in people.

Linked activities

1.6, 1.7, 1.9, 4.2, 4.8

Further reading

See 1.9.

1.10 | Case study: Combining global and local

Two large vehicle manufacturers – one from Sweden, the other from the USA – have set up a joint venture to produce trucks worldwide.

In a very competitive, low-margin market, they have two objectives:

A to minimise costs and maximise efficiency

B to develop strong sales and a positive image in a wide range of developed and developing markets.

They decide on a number of steps to achieve these objectives.

1 Read the actions 1–12 below, and write A or B in each box, depending on which of the above objectives is being followed.

2 Add any further actions you consider useful, and rank the final list in order of priority.

---

1 Encourage managers to speak at least two languages, and to understand at least one more. ☐

2 Run briefing sessions to make managers aware of the diversity of the market and of the workforce. ☐

3 Standardise and share logistical systems with their parent companies. ☐

4 Source and purchase materials and components together, using the resources of the parent companies. ☐

5 Encourage innovative products for each market. ☐

6 Have a strong local marketing force which identifies national and local needs and preferences, and adapts the standard products to them. ☐

7 Manufacture standard platforms as a basis for all their vehicles. ☐

8 Mass produce all components which are not seen by the customer. ☐

9 Set up a number of focus groups to examine customer requirements. ☐

10 Organise seminars on customer-focused business. ☐

11 Make sure that top and middle management all work for some time in countries other than their own. ☐

12 Organise seminars for middle management to examine the challenge of working with colleagues and customers from a wide range of cultural backgrounds. ☐

Aims
• To focus on the range of cultures which can influence an individual's behaviour.

Procedure

1 Ask students which cultures they feel they are influenced by: how their ideas and their behaviour are moulded to some extent by the people and events around them. Include large groups such as nationality, and also smaller ones such as clubs or teams.

2 Look at the culture onion and ask if other layers could be added in addition to those already discussed. Possibilities include geographical regions within a country, social class, departments within a company and work teams.

3 Form groups to discuss task 2. Ask each group to rank the relative importance of the different cultures mentioned so far, in shaping people's ideas and behaviour. At this stage they should be thinking in general terms, although of course every person is a unique product of different influences, including individually inherited characteristics. Thinking generally should help recognise and avoid the danger of stereotyping. Compare results through a spokesperson from each group, and encourage discussion.

4 Introduce task 3. Ask the groups to choose a person whom they can briefly analyse in terms of how representative they are of the cultural groups they belong to. Ask a spokesperson to report back from each group, and encourage discussion.

Outcomes

This activity should encourage students to consider how far we are a product of our different cultures, and how far we are unique individuals. It should also allow them to reflect on the complex cultural situations in which we all live and work.

Development

Culture is normally associated with the place where you were born or have spent most of your life, usually a country. This is because countries often share vital characteristics such as history, climate, laws, art or geography. But there are other groups which have their own distinctive cultures, for example:

• a larger geographical area:
  south-east Asia, North America, southern Europe

• a part of a country:
  California, Siberia, western Norway, Yorkshire
• a company:
  IBM, Ericsson, Nissan, Alcatel
• a team:
  China Sea project team, new software implementation project
• a function:
  mechanical engineers, financial controllers
• a professional association:
  the American Institute of Certified Public Accountants, the British Medical Association.

At the centre of all these groups is the individual, whose combination of inherited genes and specific environmental influences have made him or her a unique person.

This individual will be a member of many different cultures.

At the same time as sharing some of the characteristics of each of these groups, he or she as an individual will have much in common with people outside the same groups.

Categories will inevitably overlap: a Colombian employee of Ericsson may derive certain cultural characteristics from his or her country and others from the company. The former could make him or her different from an Ericsson employee in Britain; the latter could make him or her different from a Colombian working for Siemens.

Linked activities

2.5, 2.7, 2.8, 3.1, 6.4

Further reading

The many influences that colour our acts of communication are thoroughly analysed in

Communicating with Strangers (4th Edition), by William B. Gudykunst and Young Yun Kim, 2002, New York: McGraw-Hill.

For valuable insights into the dimensions of national culture and how these affect societies, institutions and the workplace, see

Cultures and Organizations: Software of the Mind, by Geert Hofstede and Gert Jan Hofstede, 2004 Third Millennium Edition, New York: McGraw-Hill.

2.1 The culture onion

The onion shows five different layers of culture which might affect an individual's identity:

- Local community
- Profession/occupation
- Company
- Business sector
- Country

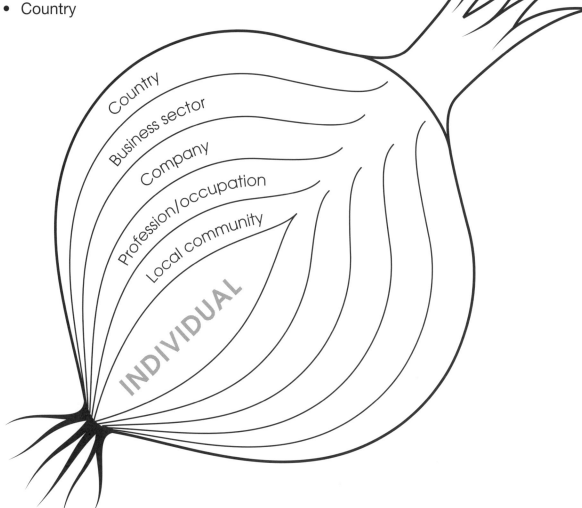

1 Can you add other layers to the onion?
2 Which layers of culture do you think are the most influential on a person's behaviour?
3 Choose a person you know quite well and explain how he or she has been influenced by the different cultures he or she belongs to.

Aims

• To show that sports possess cultural characteristics which influence the people who play them.
• To focus on the team cultures of certain sports.

Procedure

1 Ask the class about their own experiences of sport, whether as an individual or as a member of a team, and ask them to describe the people they play with. Together with the physical characteristics they mention (strength, speed, etc.), try to include some non-physical characteristics such as patience and versatility. Students who play different sports should be asked to compare the different qualities required, for instance, for tennis and skiing. Encourage students to look at the distinction between the individuals who play particular sports and the clubs, teams and associations involved in the same sport.

2 Introduce task 1, checking that the list of characteristics is understood. In pairs or small groups, ask students to choose a sport which is familiar to most members of the group, and to suggest three characteristics from the list. (Other characteristics may be added if desired.) Those who claim to play no sport at all should be encouraged to draw on their impressions gained from the media. Ask a spokesperson from each group to call out the characteristics or list them on the board. Encourage discussion.

3 Task 2 concentrates on the team aspect, and tries to identify why some teams are more successful than others. Certain sports such as athletics and golf may be seen as mainly individual sports, but most of them can be seen to have teams at national level. Ask students for a few examples of local, regional or international teams which have had success, and speculate as to why this is so. Ask pairs or small groups to draw up their list, and to report on their results. During feedback, encourage them to spot points of agreement between groups, and any similarities between sports, such as the need for cooperation in figure skating and sailing.

Outcomes

Two points may emerge from this activity:

• People who play certain sports will often develop attitudes and behaviour similar to those of the people they play with.
• By sharing certain characteristics with colleagues, individuals can cooperate successfully as a team.

Development

Many students will relate easily to sport, others less so. In discussion, encourage students to consider how the idea of teams can relate to areas other than sport, such as business, where departments or project teams can benefit from sharing cultural characteristics.

Linked activities

2.1, 2.5, 4.2

Further reading

Little has been written about sport as a cultural phenomenon, but a good start has been made in
The Rites of Men: Manhood, Politics and the Culture of Sport, by Varda Burstyn, 1999, Toronto: University of Toronto Press.

2.2 Sport and teams

Sports have their own sets of cultural characteristics, and these characteristics have an impact on the identities of individuals, teams and clubs involved in them.

1 Choose a sport from the list below, and identify three characteristics which you associate with people who practise it.

Sport	Characteristics
Athletics: • 4 x 100m relay • pole vault • marathon Baseball Basketball Boxing Downhill skiing Figure skating Golf Ice hockey Motor racing Mountaineering Rowing Rugby Sailing Soccer Squash Tennis: • doubles • singles	Ability to take criticism Aggression Calmness Cooperation Determination to practise Egotism Extroversion Patience Perseverance Quick thinking Sensitivity Sharing Stamina Teamwork Toughness Versatility

2 For three of these sports:
   • choose a successful team
   • discuss the characteristics which have contributed to the success of the team.

Procedure

1 The role of gender in society is a big and potentially controversial topic. Try to limit the scope of this activity by focusing on communication, and by explaining that 'masculine' and 'feminine' are labels used to identify two broad clusters of characteristics rather than to describe the way all men and all women communicate. Open up discussion by asking students what they understand by the two terms when applied to communicating styles.

2 The first two paragraphs should help summarise this discussion. Make sure the list in task 1 is clearly understood, and ask students to work in groups to separate them into the predominantly masculine and predominantly feminine. Explain that there is no absolutely 'correct' division (some of the words may be interpreted in different ways) but that certain trends may appear. Compare results through a spokesperson from each group, and discuss how far they conform to a regular pattern. If desired, copy the list in Outcomes onto the board or flipchart or onto an overhead transparency. Compare this list with theirs and discuss any differences.

3 Depending on the students in your class, decide with them whether they should discuss national or corporate culture in tasks 2 and 3. Students should work in pairs or small groups and try to decide in general terms whether the culture in question is predominantly masculine or feminine, based on the qualities suggested above, and whether they would prefer it to be otherwise. Ask a spokesperson from each group to describe results, and encourage discussion.

Outcomes

The following division is offered merely as a guideline drawn from a mainly British or European standpoint: there is obviously scope for different interpretations of some of the words. For example, cooperating could be seen as a strong element of male teamwork or as an important part of female supportive collaboration. The important thing is that students form a clear idea of choices and variety in communicating styles.

Feminine	Masculine
Advising	Challenging
Affiliating	Competing
Asking	Contesting
Communicating	Correcting
Confirming	Criticising
Consulting	Directing
Cooperating	Humiliating
Empathising	Informing
Enquiring	Ordering
Networking	Protesting
Reconciling	Reacting
Sharing	Solving

Development

There is a considerable body of specialist and popular literature on this subject, on which most people have strong opinions. Discussion should follow quite easily, and one of your main roles may be to contain it within the confines described above.

Linked activities

2.4, 2.5, 6.3, 6.9

Further reading

See chapter 4 ('He, she and (s)he') for background on the cultural constructs of masculinity and femininity in

Cultures and Organizations: Software of the Mind, by Geert Hofstede and Gert Jan Hofstede, 2004 Third Millennium Edition, New York: McGraw-Hill.

Gender can play a fundamental role in defining the identity of an individual or the culture of a group.

Certain companies or groups are said to have characteristics which are predominantly masculine or predominantly feminine. These characteristics tend to be based on a general view of the roles of men and women, rather than the notion that 'men/women always do this'.

1 Based on your own feeling for what is 'masculine' and what is 'feminine', divide the following actions or characteristics into those you would describe as predominantly masculine and those you would describe as predominantly feminine. Put M or F by each one.

Advising	❑	Directing	❑
Affiliating	❑	Empathising	❑
Asking	❑	Enquiring	❑
Challenging	❑	Humiliating	❑
Communicating	❑	Informing	❑
Competing	❑	Networking	❑
Confirming	❑	Ordering	❑
Consulting	❑	Protesting	❑
Contesting	❑	Reacting	❑
Cooperating	❑	Reconciling	❑
Correcting	❑	Sharing	❑
Criticising	❑	Solving	❑

2 Would you describe your own culture (national or corporate) as predominantly masculine or predominantly feminine?

3 Which of the above characteristics would you wish to be more evident, and which less evident in your own organisation?

Aims

- To show that gender can have an impact on communication style.
- To identify sources of potential conflict when different styles meet.

Procedure

1 Ask students to reflect on conversations which they have had with people in the past. Ask them what makes a successful conversation, and why some conversations are not successful. Ask if they think mixed groups of men and women have more difficulty than single-gender groups. If so, why? This could suggest that each gender has a different style of communication. Try to avoid stereotyping by explaining that 'masculine' and 'feminine' refer to styles of communicating rather than to a division between the sexes. Many people have a blend of these two sets of characteristics.

2 Check that students understand the introduction and four dialogues, and explain that in task 1 they have to identify which of the speakers in each dialogue has a more masculine style and which a more feminine one. Ask them to do the activity in pairs or small groups, then compare answers and discuss the results.

3 Explain task 2: to identify the main differences in style of the two characters. Students may use their own words, but those given in Outcomes could be given as examples.

Outcomes

The most common categorisation is:

1 A feminine, B masculine
2 A masculine, B feminine
3 A feminine, B masculine
4 A feminine, B masculine

A successful conversation requires listening, showing respect, showing understanding and interest, sympathising and turn taking. Body language, facial expression and eye contact are also very important.

Breakdowns in effective communication occur because:

1 A is cooperating, consulting, reconciling; B is contesting, correcting, challenging.
2 A is challenging; B is enquiring, empathising.
3 A is asking; B is directing, ordering.
4 A is asking, communicating, enquiring; B is competing, informing, contesting.

Development

Ask for more examples of the kind of breakdown shown in these dialogues, from life and from fiction. Ask students to rephrase the dialogues so that more positive communication results.

Linked activities

2.3, 2.5, 6.1

Further reading

For the effects of gender on communication, see *Gender and Discourse*, by Deborah Tannen, 1996, Oxford: Oxford University Press.

2.4 Gender and communication

People with very different communication styles often have difficulty developing a real understanding. Two styles which can produce conflict come from so-called 'masculine' and 'feminine' cultures. The terms do not necessarily relate to all men and all women, but are used to denote characteristics often seen to be typical of each gender.

Read the following dialogues.
1 Identify A and B as 'masculine' or 'feminine'.
2 Summarise the difference in approach of the two people.

1

A: There's a good film on television this evening, it's about a mad doctor.
B: Yes, I know. He's not mad actually, just eccentric.
A: There was a good review of it in the newspaper yesterday.
B: It was on Monday. I remember, I read it on the train.
A: It sounds quite interesting.
B: Yes, not quite so good as that one we saw about ghosts last week.
A: It would be something different from what we usually see, that will be nice.
B: Really? I thought we saw a film about a mad doctor just a few weeks ago.

2

A: Morning.
B: Morning, how are you feeling today?
A: I'm OK. Why do you ask?

3

A: What time do we take off tomorrow?
B: Be ready by 10.30.

4

A: ... and what do you do?
B: I'm a product development manager, working mainly in the area of bearings for the automotive industry. I'm responsible for development worldwide, so I travel quite a lot, especially in south-east Asia. How about you?
A: I'm a journalist.
B: Oh, my brother's a journalist, he's freelance, but he works a lot for the New York Herald. He's done that for quite a few years now ...
A: Oh, that sounds interesting.
B: Yes, it is, but it has its boring moments. I could have been a journalist too, but I was good at engineering ...

Aims

- To illustrate the existence of stereotypes.
- To explore whether there is any legitimate basis to national stereotyping.

Procedure

1 Ask the class what is meant by stereotype (an exaggerated, often uncomplimentary view of someone from another culture), and ask for examples. It should not be too difficult to establish that the most common stereotypes are often untypical of the group they portray, and almost always out of date. But it may be possible to argue that there is an element of truth in some of them: the challenge is not to apply a blanket description to a whole group of people.

2 Introduce task 1, and ask pairs or groups to match the two columns. Compare each group's results, and tell them the results in Outcomes below. Discuss any discrepancies and consider to what extent these national stereotypes are justified and to what extent they are inaccurate.

3 Introduce task 2. Form pairs or small groups to come up with some examples of stereotypes. Ask a volunteer from each group to summarise the feelings of their group. Encourage a class discussion as to the validity of these stereotypes.

4 Finally, ask students to reflect and comment on stereotypical views of their own national culture.

Outcomes

The stereotypes suggested:

British – hypocritical
Germans – arrogant
Italians – cowardly
Spaniards – lazy
Swedes – sex-mad

This activity should allow an open discussion on the danger of stereotyping and to what extent it makes cooperation difficult between different nations. It should not be difficult to prove that it is unlikely for all the inhabitants of one country to have one over-riding characteristic.

Development

It may be interesting to consider where certain stereotypes originated. The idea that all Swedes are sex-mad probably had some link with Ingmar Bergman's films, and that Scots people are said to be mean probably originated from a time when food was very scarce. It could also be interesting to mention individuals who go completely against the stereotype, such as 'the shy Italian' or 'the talkative Japanese'. Other examples can be given from the students' own national culture or cultures.

Linked activities

1.5, 1.8, 2.6, 2.7, 2.8

Further reading

For the genesis and functions of stereotypes and prejudice and their effects on attitude, see pp. 169–205, chapter 6 ('Intergroup Relations: Cultures in Contact') in

Understanding Culture's Influence on Behavior (2nd Edition), by Richard Brislin, 1999, Fort Worth: Harcourt Brace Jovanovich.

2.5 | Stereotyping

Sexism, racism, ageism and religious intolerance are examples of prejudice which are only too frequently observed. Another form of prejudice is stereotyping, which occurs when someone claims that members of another culture all share the same, often inferior or offensive characteristics.

A recent report from the European Union listed some of the national perceptions which make cooperation difficult.

1 Match each of the nationalities with the stereotype you think is often attached to it:

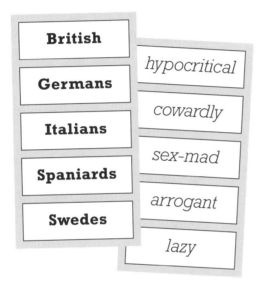

British

Germans

Italians

Spaniards

Swedes

hypocritical

cowardly

sex-mad

arrogant

lazy

2 Which nationalities are stereotypically associated with the following characteristics?
- Obsessed with fashion
- Slow-thinking
- Insincere
- Obsessed with tradition
- Mean
- Reserved
- Obsessed with food

Aims

- To recognise the kinds of attitude commonly held towards other cultures.
- To evaluate these attitudes.

Procedure

1 Introduce the idea of different attitudes to other cultures by asking students about attitudes they have met. Students should be brief. Don't allow them to begin long anecdotal stories. Limit discussion to a few minutes at this stage.

2 Students should read the statements. Check that they understand the sentences and what they have to do in task 1. Get them to fill in their responses individually. They should then work in small groups and compare and contrast their responses.

3 A spokesperson for each group should then summarise the results for the rest of the class. Compare and discuss these, and see if there is some sort of consensus.

4 Tasks 2 and 3: individually, students should now select their 'best' and 'worst' statements and be prepared to justify them.

5 As a class activity, invite individuals to present their 'best' and 'worst' statements, explaining and justifying their choices. Invite comment and discussion.

Outcomes

The reactions of individual students to these statements will obviously differ. There is room for a good deal of disagreement, so it is not necessary to look for a consensus. However, it would be useful for students to pick out those with which they agree and formulate a short description of what they know and think about culture and attitudes in general.

Development

Students may like to consider which of the statements show a helpful approach to formulating attitudes towards culture in general and other cultures in particular. Some, such as 9 and 12, could be said to be negative, while 8, 13 and 14, for example, suggest flexibility and tolerance.

Linked activities

2.5, 2.7, 2.8, 4.8, 6.12

Further reading

See 2.5.

2.6 Evaluating attitudes

How do you form your attitudes towards people from other cultures? Do you expect them to be very different from you? Do you think of them as all being the same? Are you aware of how you appear to them?

1 Read the statements below and show how much you agree or disagree by putting the appropriate number in the box:

5 = Agree strongly   4 = Agree   3 = No opinion   2 = Disagree   1 = Disagree strongly

> **1** *Observation of different cultures allows us to form patterns.*

> **8** *We must learn to recognise the existence of different but equally valid styles.*

> **2** *I don't wish to be classified. I am an individual.*

> **9** *Different is dangerous.*

> **3** *Generalisations capture similarities and hide differences.*

> **10** *The fish is the last one to recognise the water.*

> **4** *Regarding people of the same culture as all being the same is harmful and dangerous.*

> **11** *Statistical facts about cultures help us classify them.*

> **5** *People from other cultures often act strangely.*

> **12** *Other people don't try to adapt enough.*

> **6** *Ignoring the differences between cultures is dangerous.*

> **13** *One man's meat is another man's poison.*

> **7** *We can categorise certain groups of people according to how they behave.*

> **14** *Beauty is in the eye of the beholder.*

2 Select the statement which most appeals to you, and justify it with examples.

3 Decide which one you find least accurate.

2.7 | The bell-jar graph

Aims
- To show how generalisations about cultures may have a certain statistical validity.
- To show that they can also be highly misleading.

Procedure

1 Ask students to give examples of a typical stereotype close to their own experience. It could be a national stereotype, or a professional one such as a very serious judge. Then ask if this means that all judges are serious. The generalisation that judges are serious could be true, but that does not mean to say that the next judge you come into contact with will be serious. This is what the bell-graph illustrates: statistical probability, together with the possibility of exceptions.

2 Check that students understand the general idea of the graph and the four figures shown: two 'stereotypes' and two 'exceptions'.

3 Explain task 1. Students should work in pairs or small groups to put together a description of the graph, explaining in their own words the existence of both stereotypes and exceptions. Each group then presents their results, followed by questioning, comment and discussion.

4 Move on to tasks 2 and 3, in which pairs or small groups discuss which cultures could be used as examples of the graph shown. In Europe, for example, the Italians are often characterised as emotional, and the Finns as reserved. Ask each group to give its examples, then discuss whether everybody else agrees.

5 A further test may be to apply the bell-jar idea to the culture or cultures of the students themselves. In both cases, study the validity of the generalisation and look for examples of exceptions.

Outcomes

When thinking of specific cultures, be careful to distinguish between a general statement based on statistics and likelihood, on the one hand, and specific cases on the other. The latter can be very different from the former, and students should be ready to meet the 'exception' as well as the 'stereotype'.

Development

Discussion could lead on to how one prepares for meeting members of other cultures: whether to assume that most people will be typical of their culture, or be ready to meet many exceptions. Both stances will be useful; the important thing is to keep both in mind.

Linked activities

2.5, 2.6, 2.8

Further reading

The difference between stereotype and generalisation is explained by Milton J. Bennett in his article 'Intercultural Communication: A Current Perspective' in

Basic Concepts of Intercultural Communication: Selected Readings, edited by Milton J. Bennett, 1998, Yarmouth: Intercultural Press.

2.7 | The bell-jar graph

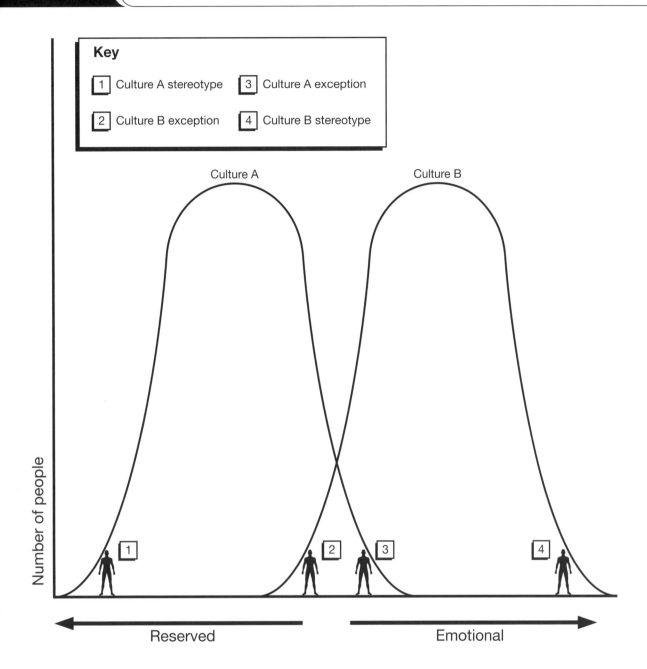

Key

| 1 | Culture A stereotype | 3 | Culture A exception |
| 2 | Culture B exception | 4 | Culture B stereotype |

Culture A

Culture B

Number of people

Reserved

Emotional

The graph shows the range of positions of two cultures, A and B, on a scale ranging from reserved to emotional.

1 Study the graph and explain how it helps break down stereotypical ideas about members of other groups.
2 Give examples of cultures which are similar to A.
3 Give examples of cultures which are similar to B.

2.8 | Where do stereotypes come from?

Aims

• To discover some of the forces which cause people to adopt stereotypical attitudes.
• To assess their relative importance.

Procedure

1 Ask students if they can imagine the landscape and the people of a country they have never visited. Ask them how they gathered these impressions. The landscape can be seen in photos, but there may be a variety of inputs about people, such as films and books, or friends who have made a visit. Ask if there is a possibility of getting prejudiced or one-sided views from these.

2 Ask students to look at the list and, working in pairs or groups, to do task 1, adding any other influences they can think of. If so, quickly add these to the list.

3 Set the pairs or groups to work on task 2. Within each group they should try to come to some agreement, in order to promote discussion. Each group then appoints a spokesperson to explain what they chose and why. Encourage comment and discussion.

Outcomes

Many different outcomes are possible, but students should increase their understanding of how attitudes are formed in themselves and in other people.

Development

Ask students to evaluate their own attitudes to other cultures in general or to any specific one, and to try to find out where they came from. Encourage comparison between students.

Linked activities

2.5, 2.6, 6.4

Further reading

See 2.7.

Stereotypes usually involve negative views of other cultures. How are they formed?

1 Look at the list below and add any influences you think are missing.

2 Select the four which you consider most common.

> Inherited characteristics
>
> Parents and family
>
> The media
>
> Friends
>
> Education (school, university)
>
> Inferiority complexes
>
> The neighbourhood
>
> Clubs and societies
>
> Religion
>
> Travel
>
> Laziness
>
> Fear
>
> A sense of superiority
>
> Limited imagination
>
> Lack of experience of people
>
> Poor communication skills
>
> Envy

Aims
- To identify some of the factors that can shape a national culture.
- To show the difference between describing your own national culture and describing somebody else's.

Procedure

1 Ask students for ideas on the main factors which shape and define different national cultures. Encourage them to include attitudes and institutions as well as the more obvious behavioural aspects.

2 Explain that they should study the lists and do task 1 in pairs or groups, adding or removing any items they think necessary. If they have no suggestions, move quickly on to task 2.

3 The aim of task 2 is, with the help of the lists, to provide useful information for a visitor to a given country. Each student should consider their own country and another one; in multicultural classes this will mean forming pairs, but larger groups can be formed in less varied classes. You may prefer to ask students to select the three or four most important factors. Feedback through a spokesperson should pick out which factors are important, and how the visitor can benefit from being aware of them.

Outcomes

Focus on the difference between describing aspects of your own national culture and those of another. Did students find it easier to do one than the other. Also ask students to identify any differences between how they see their own national culture and how others see it. Is one view more critical than another? Were they surprised by the (in)accuracy of other people's views? There should be a variety of responses here, leading to discussion.

Development

Ask the class to develop their ideas into a more generalised description of their own national culture, still focusing on the key factors. This is similar to the exercise in 3.4; here it may also be applied to a culture other than the student's own.

Linked activities

3.3, 3.4

Further reading

A short discussion of how cultures originate can be found in pp. 25–8 in

Culture's Consequences: Comparing values, behaviors, institutions and organizations across nations, by Geert Hofstede, 2001 2nd Edition, Thousand Oaks, CA: Sage Publications.

See also

The Silent Language, by E.T. Hall, 1997, New York: Anchor Books.

3.1 | Cultural influences

National cultures are formed and influenced by a wide range of factors.

The lists below contain some of these factors, grouped into three main categories: structural, social and physical.

STRUCTURAL

Geography

Communications

Climate

Population density and spread

Centralisation of power

Role of religion

Political system

Role of authority

SOCIAL

Balance between family and work

Class distinctions

Dress

Punctuality

Emotional displays

Ideas of physical beauty

Taboos

Humour

Respect for age

Gender

Politeness to the outsider

PHYSICAL

Physical contact

Physical gestures

Physical distance

Speech: volume, speed

Handshakes and greetings

Body language

1 Look through the lists and make any improvements you think necessary: add items which are missing, and take away any which you consider to be unimportant.

2 Try to decide which of these factors are important in shaping:
- your own national or regional culture
- another culture which you know well.

3.2 | Body language

Aims
- To show how certain physical actions are more acceptable than others in different cultures.
- To define what is and is not acceptable in different situations.

Procedure

1 Ask students to think of certain physical actions which annoy them, such as people who speak loudly, or gesticulate excessively, or stand close to you when they speak. Discuss whether the same actions are annoying to everyone, and whether they would be more acceptable in some cultures than in others. You may also consider the attitudes of people from other cultural backgrounds to greetings, such as handshakes, bows, kisses and hugs.

2 Introduce task 1, checking understanding of the actions and of the instructions. Working in pairs or small groups, encourage students to agree on one response, rather than say 'It depends'. Encourage them also to give graphic examples of what is or is not acceptable, such as a gentle and an over-vigorous scratch of the head. This should provide some light relief.

3 Move on to task 2 and ask for feedback and encourage comparison and discussion.

4 If the question has not already arisen, ask the class whether their answers would be different if they were referring to an informal situation such as a group of friends at a social gathering. This would help to show that within the same national culture there can be enormously different norms for different social settings.

Outcomes

Encourage students to consider whether the actions can be divided into three groups:
- generally unacceptable, such as yawning
- generally acceptable, such as nodding your head
- variable, depending on how you do it, such as hands on hips.

This will not necessarily bring consensus, but will encourage experimentation and discussion.

Development

Students could be encouraged to think about what actions are generally considered unacceptable in their own country. This could lead to a discussion of possible taboos, such as the discussion of death, cannibalism, or incest, and how these are changing.

Students could also consider and discuss whether there are any actions in their country which are acceptable for men but not for women.

Linked activities

5.5, 6.12

Further reading

For an amusing survey of body language across the globe, see

Gestures: The Do's and Taboos of Body Language Around the World, by Roger Axtell, 1997, New York: John Wiley.

3.2 Body language

Different physical signals mean different things to different people, depending on factors such as nationality, status and situation.

1 Look at the list of physical actions below. Put the appropriate number in the box to say if in your national culture they are:

1 = perfectly acceptable   2 = just about acceptable

3 = unacceptable in a formal situation such as a business meeting

2 Choose a culture other than your own and decide which of the actions would be in a different category.

①	laughing loudly	☐
②	scratching your head	☐
③	touching somebody on the arm as you speak to them	☐
④	looking somebody straight in the eye for 5 seconds or more	☐
⑤	sitting with your legs wide apart	☐
⑥	adjusting your clothing: tie, bra, trouser belt	☐
⑦	moving close to someone	☐
⑧	standing with hands on hips	☐
⑨	crossing your arms	☐
⑩	putting your feet on the table	☐
⑪	not looking at someone when you speak to them	☐
⑫	yawning	☐
⑬	whispering to a colleague	☐
⑭	nodding your head emphatically	☐
⑮	blowing your nose	☐
⑯	smoking	☐

3.3 | Time capsule

Aims

- To get students to reflect on the main characteristics of the contemporary culture of their country.
- To evaluate some of those characteristics.

Procedure

1 Raise the idea of a time capsule, and ask for any examples of regional, national or international time capsules. Explain that the purpose of this activity is to devise one for a specific culture.

2 Check that students understand the task, and clarify which culture is to be described. In monocultural classes this should be the 'home' culture, but in multicultural classes the target culture will have to be negotiated between the pairs or groups doing the task.

Encourage students to bring in examples of the things they decide on, or to make drawings or bring photos. They should give their feedback as a group presentation using these visuals.

Outcomes

The result of the activity should be an interesting presentation, or a display using objects and visuals.

Development

The same exercise could be applied to other national cultures.

Introduce the element of personal choice by asking students to choose the three things they most like about their national culture, and the three things they least like about it. This could lead to a discussion on the quality of life in a particular country today.

Linked activities

1.4, 3.1, 3.4

Further reading

For a classification of a given culture, E.T. Hall refers to the manipulation of the physical world as 'exploitation' in pp. 196–7, 'Map of Culture' in *The Silent Language*, by E.T. Hall, 1997, New York: Anchor Books.

3.3 | Time capsule

Some aspects of culture change quite quickly, others change more slowly.

Imagine you have been commissioned to devise a time capsule which, in one thousand years' time, will give a clear idea of the culture of your country at the beginning of the 21st century. Try to make the capsule as representative as possible of the things that shape or have shaped your national culture today. Include ten items, only one of which may be a book.

Possible categories:
- Technology
- Fashion
- Art
- Leisure
- Literature
- Customs
- Behaviour
- Demonstrations
- Politics and politicians

Which country?

3.4 Family briefing

Aims
- To encourage students to take a detailed look at a national culture they know.
- To be able to describe a national culture in practical terms for a visitor.

Procedure

1 Ask students about visits they have made to other countries, and how far they have found it useful to prepare themselves in advance. How much information is useful and/or necessary, either for a holiday or for a period of residence? This activity will give practice in preparing that kind of advice.

2 Check that task 1 is clear, and that the list of suggestions is understood in the same way by everybody. Wherever possible, the target culture should be the student's own, but in multicultural groups some will contribute as 'outsiders'. The list of suggestions given can be added to in a quick brainstorming session. Then students should do the task in pairs or small groups. They should select their main headings, then prepare a few notes under each one.

3 Introduce task 2 by asking whether you would need to point out to a German that business people in Belgium shake hands when they first meet. Then explore how much explanation might be needed for the way people greet each other in other countries – particularly ones which are further away. Ask students to compile a list of aspects of their own national culture that might surprise people from other countries.

4 Ask for feedback in the form of group mini-presentations followed by questions and discussion.

Outcomes

The feedback session – a form of cultural briefing (see activities 1.4 and 1.5) – should show how some types of information can be useful preparation for a visit to or residence in another country.

Development

Discuss what kinds of information are most useful in this situation. Some may be very practical, such as public transport. Others, such as social relations, may be more open to different interpretations and therefore varied, depending on the informant.

Linked activities

1.4, 1.5, 3.1, 3.2, 3.3

Further reading

Background information on the problems involved when entire families move abroad can be found in pp. 264–81, 'Social Support and the Challenges of International Assignments: Implications for Trainers', by Gary Fontaine in

Handbook of Intercultural Training (2nd Edition), edited by D. Landis and R.S. Bhagat, 1996, Thousand Oaks: Sage Publications, Inc.

3.4 | Family briefing

1 A family of four (parents and two teenage children) are about to move to your country for a period of five years. Prepare some information and advice. Think about these categories, among others:

SERVICES

public transport
education
housing
shops and shopping
bureaucracy

SOCIAL

entertaining
visiting
clubs and societies
sport and leisure
religion
clothing
home life
street life
formality / informality
currency and prices

WORK

working hours
dress
formality of address
written / verbal styles
punctuality

2 Would certain types of information be more useful for some cultures or nationalities than for others? If so, give examples.

Aims

- To illustrate some of the dimensions used to describe corporate culture.
- To find examples of companies exemplifying these dimensions.

Procedure

1 Ask students if they think that different companies have different profiles or cultures – that is, different ways of behaving and doing business. Some students may have a wide experience to draw on, but if not, ask them to contrast what it must be like working for a small local firm compared with a large multinational food company. Try to include mention of some of the dimensions listed in the activity. You could also point out that companies in the same business sectors (such as banking, software development, or the automotive industry) also share certain cultural characteristics.

2 Explain the activity, which is a simple matching exercise. To make it easier, start with the example given. Then tell students, working in pairs or groups, to start with the dimensions they find easiest (1 and 8, perhaps), and do the matching through a process of elimination.

Compare results through a spokesperson from each group, and try to introduce examples of each dimension as it is identified.

3 Task 2 may be more successful with students who have some experience of international business, but can still be done by the less experienced, based on their perceptions of different companies, both international and local. If possible, try to place experienced students in a group with those who are less experienced. The task should lead to discussion about what it is like to work in different types of company.

Outcomes

The matchings are: 1 f, 2 a, 3 d, 4 h, 5 e, 6 c, 7 g, 8 b.

Where there is disagreement, ask students to explain the correct choice. It would be possible, for example, to describe relationships with colleagues (7) as formal or informal (b), but this would cause problems with impersonal or personal (g).

Development

Background reading from Recommended reading on page 9 or from Further reading below could be a useful addition to this activity.

Linked activities

4.2, 4.3, 4.5, 4.6, 4.7

Further reading

See

Mind Your Manners, by John Mole (3rd Edition), 2003, London: Nicholas Brealey

for practical suggestions for assessing the cultural matrix of a company's communication, organisation and leadership.

An essential read for a more in-depth account of the effect of culture on corporations is

Cultures and Organizations: Software of the Mind, by Geert Hofstede and Gert Jan Hofstede, 2004 Third Millennium Edition, New York: McGraw-Hill.

4.1 Company dimensions

All companies have their own unique culture. The culture of an international company is often strongly influenced by the culture of the parent company. Subsidiaries often display a mixture of characteristics, some coming from headquarters and some from the local culture.

The list on the left below shows some of the dimensions which can be used to define company culture. On the right are two extreme points for each of the same dimensions, but in a different order.

1 Match each dimension with the pair which suits it best.
For example: Planning perspective (3) is best described as long-term or short-term (d).

1 Image of leader	**a** hierarchical *or* flat
2 Company structure	**b** formal *or* informal
3 Planning perspective	**c** normative, based on rules *or* pragmatic, depending on the situation
4 Timing of activities	**d** long-term *or* short-term
5 Basis for status in company	**e** who you are *or* what you do
6 Decision-making process	**f** strong individual *or* leader of group
7 Relationships with colleagues	**g** impersonal *or* personal
8 Dress codes	**h** sequential/monochronic (one activity at a time) *or* synchronic/polychronic (several activities at the same time)

2 Give examples of any companies you know which display cultural characteristics of types shown in the right-hand column (for example, a company with a strict, formal dress code).

4.2 | Brand, image and culture

Aims
- To see whether a company's brand image can be related to its culture.
- To identify important cultural characteristics of some well-known companies.

Procedure

1 Ask students what springs to mind when they think of certain big companies, such as media companies, or makers of food or drink, sports equipment, computers or household furnishings. They might think of young people, fashionable clothes, healthy bodies, social acceptability, or the character of the head of the company. Try to bring in some of the characteristics listed in the activity. You may also wish to mention other characteristics, such as:

aggressive marketing
worker participation
discipline
respect for colleagues
identification through products
strong customer focus
good internal communications
traditional products
traditional image
technological innovation
good design
long history
shareholder value
environmental friendliness
advertising designed to shock

Discuss whether companies make an effort to appeal to certain types of market or customer by the way they present themselves to the public, and also by the way they are organised and the way they behave internally. Also, encourage students to think about the distinction between the culture of a company and the image the company wants to project.

2 Introduce task 1, asking students to choose, in their pairs or groups, a company which they know well. Alternatively, they may each choose a different company. In each case, ask them to report back to the class the characteristics they have identified, adding, if possible, an overall view of the company and whether they find its image attractive.

3 Do task 2 in a similar way, preferably with a smaller, local company, in order to create a contrast. After feedback, see if there has been a big difference in perceptions between the first company and the second.

Outcomes

A link may be seen between the way a company produces or encourages a certain culture in its own organisation, and the image it wishes to project in public, to help it sell its products.

Development

Suggestions for further reading are given below.

You may choose to discuss more generally the use of brands as a marketing tool designed to attract a certain part of the market. Sport sponsorship, TV campaigns, merchandising, press releases, logos and other devices could be mentioned, together perhaps with some of the things companies may wish to hide, such as accusations of exploitation and excessive profits.

Linked activities

4.1, 4.4, 4.5, 4.6, 4.7, 4.8

Further reading

For more information on the challenges of marketing in a cross-cultural context, see

Marketing Across Cultures, by Fons Trompenaars and Peter Woolliams, 2003, New York: John Wiley.

4.2 Brand, image and culture

Some large companies 'brand' themselves by creating an image which many people recognise. This brand helps customers to identify and remember the company and its products. Brands can be related to the culture of the company, but brand, image and culture are not always closely linked.

1 From the list of companies below, choose one you know reasonably well. Identify the characteristics which most help to identify its culture and develop its brand image. The list of characteristics may be useful.

Companies

Jack Daniels	IKEA
IBM	Gucci
BP Amoco	Ericsson
Levi	Fabergé
Cisco Systems	Zanussi
Monsanto	Microsoft
GAP	Time Warner
Sony	Ben & Jerry's
Apple	Nokia

Characteristics

- Image of leader: strong individual *or* team person
- Company structure: hierarchical *or* flat
- Planning perspective: long-term *or* short-term
- Basis for status in company: who you are *or* what you do
- Decision-making process: normative, based on rules *or* pragmatic, depending on the situation
- Relationships with colleagues: impersonal or personal
- Dress codes: formal *or* informal

2 Choose another company that you know well. Describe it by selecting its most important characteristics, as above.

Aims

- To show how the way the telephone is used by employees forms part of a company's culture.
- To devise a suitable telephone style for the students' own national culture.

Procedure

1 Ask students for examples of telephone phrases and habits which annoy them, such as being cut off early or being left waiting a long time with music playing; and things which they like, such as a friendly tone of voice. Students do not need to agree on these points, but they will realise that good telephone behaviour can be influential in forming people's attitudes to a company.

2 Introduce the activity, checking that the language is understood, and explaining that the aim is to give advice appropriate to the students' own national culture. In multicultural classes this may involve covering more than one culture. Ask pairs or groups to cover the role of both call centre personnel, who work on the phone all day, especially on incoming calls, and other employees, who may phone out as much as in, and usually do not know who is phoning them when they pick up the phone.

The questions come in two parts:

General tips, with no specific language mentioned, and Use of English, in which specific examples are given. Here students may comment on the use of English by an international company they know.

3 Ask a spokesperson from each group to give feedback, and allow comment, comparison and discussion. If possible, compile on the board a list of points on which agreement has been reached.

Outcomes

Identify points of agreement and disagreement, encouraging debate. It may be possible to give amusing examples of language which students find particularly annoying, such as over-long phrases of the type: 'Good afternoon, thank you for calling Dodsworth and Sturdy, specialists in landscape development consultancy. This is Mandy your executive sales representative speaking. How may I help you?'

Development

Consider the question of standardisation: How much telephone language and style can or should be standardised? How many guidelines are necessary, if any?

Linked activities

4.8, 6.7, 6.9

Further reading

The telephone forefronts the problems of tone of voice, appropriate volume and other paralinguistic elements which convey meaning. For an introduction to the cross-cultural dimensions of communicative competence, see 'Language: Its Cultural and Intercultural Dimensions' by Alvino Fantini, in

New Ways of Teaching Culture, edited by Alvino Fantini, 1997, Alexandria, VA: TESOL.

4.3 | Case study: Telephone language

A logistics company, Logico, is about to set up business in your country. Their employees will use the phone a lot to communicate with partners and customers, so they must be as effective as possible on the telephone.

Logico already has a number of guidelines about the use of the telephone by call centre personnel and other employees, but wishes to adapt them to your country. Logico has sent out the following consultation document and your Managing Director has asked you to respond.

Give advice for:

a all employees

b call centre personnel.

General

Tone of voice:	Formal and efficient / informal and friendly?
Accents:	Avoid / encourage regional variations?
Use of names:	Always / never use first names after a certain time
Length of call:	As short as possible / depends on caller
Practical tips:	Smile as you speak / never get irritated / don't get involved with people / try to make everyone your friend

Use of English

Opening phrases:	'Logico / Good morning, Logico, this is Monica speaking, how can I help you?'
Closing phrases:	'It's been a pleasure talking to you, have a good day / Goodbye.'
Types of phrase to be avoided:	'Thanks for calling / Thanks for your time / It's been nice talking to you / Have a good day …'
Phrases to be encouraged:	'Thank you for your help.'
Examples of bad telephone technique:	Talking to someone else during your conversation

Your own favourite DOs and DON'Ts: …

Aims

- To understand the principles of Hofstede's model for describing corporate cultures.
- To illustrate attitudes and dialogue typical of the dimensions of the Hofstede model.

Procedure

1 Ask students for any experiences they have of working in different companies or organisations where things are done very differently from what they are used to. Try to introduce some of the ideas from the activity, such as the accessibility of bosses (1, c), or individualism and teamwork (3, d), and ask how this changes the atmosphere or culture of an organisation.

2 Introduce task 1, checking understanding of words and of the matching process. Encourage pairs or groups to start with the more accessible items (1 and 3, perhaps), and to collect from their experience examples of some of the characteristics described. Ask for feedback and discussion, reconciling any differences and comparing examples.

3 Introduce task 2, which relates specific language and attitudes to the dimensions. Answers are given below, but points of overlap should be used as a basis for discussion and exploration.

Outcomes

1
1 c, 2 a, 3 d, 4 e, 5 b

2
A MAS (4, e), B IDV (3, d), C PDI (1, c), D LTO (5, b), E UAI (2, a)

Development

Students who are interested may like to follow up this activity by reading parts of the Introduction to Intercultural studies at the beginning of this book. See also Further reading below.

Linked activities

4.1, 4.8, 5.5

Further reading

Standard references for Hofstede's work are

Culture's Consequences: Comparing values, behaviors, institutions and organizations across nations, by Geert Hofstede, 2001 2nd Edition, Thousand Oaks, CA: Sage Publications

and

Cultures and Organizations: Software of the Mind, by Geert Hofstede and Gert Jan Hofstede, 2004 Third Millennium Edition, New York: McGraw-Hill.

Background briefing

Geert Hofstede is the author of perhaps the most comprehensive study of culture's influence in the workplace. He analysed data collected by IBM from over 70 countries of which he first used 40; later from 50 countries plus three regions. From those results, published in his *Culture's Consequences* (2nd Edition 2001), Hofstede extrapolated a model which identifies four primary dimensions of national culture; power distance, uncertainty avoidance, individualism/collectivisim and masculinity/femininity (this last dimension tends to draw unwarranted criticism for its name alone; for a full account of this dimension, see Hofstede's *Masculinity and Femininity: The Taboo Dimension of National Cultures*, 1998).

Later work with Bond produced another dimension, Long-Term Orientation, which characterises a culture's orientation towards time, i.e. short-term or long-term (G. Hofstede and M. H. Bond, 'Confucius and economic growth: New trends in culture's consequences', in *Organizational Dynamics*, 16 (4), 4–21).

Since the completion of Hofstede's landmark study in 1973, subsequent studies of commercial airline pilots and students in 23 countries, civil service managers in 14 countries, 'up-market' consumers in 15 countries and 'elites' in 19 countries have replicated his results.

Dr Hofstede is Emeritus Professor of Organizational Anthropology and International Management at Maastricht University, and he was Senior Fellow of the Institute for Research on Intercultural Cooperation, which he co-founded in 1980, until it closed in 2004. He holds an MSc in Mechanical Engineering from Delft Technical University and a PhD in Social Psychology from the University of Groningen. He continues as Fellow of the Center for Economic Research, University of Tilburg.

Teacher's notes   4 Profiling corporate cultures

4.4 | The Hofstede model

Geert Hofstede, author of *Culture's Consequences* and *Cultures and Organizations*, uses five dimensions to describe company cultures, as listed below.

1 For each one, select the definition (a–e) which best describes it.

1 Power Distance Index (PDI)

2 Uncertainty Avoidance Index (UAI)

3 Individualism/Collectivism (IDV)

4 Masculinity/Femininity (MAS)

5 Long-Term Orientation (LTO)

a The degree to which people can:
- take risks
- accept conflict and stress
- work without rules.

b The degree to which people:
- have a short- or long-term view of their work
- accept convention
- persevere with a job
- spend or invest.

c The acceptance of the unequal distribution of power – the degree to which:
- employees are independent
- structures are hierarchical
- bosses are accessible
- people have rights or privileges
- progress is by evolution or by revolution.

d The degree to which people:
- work in groups or alone
- relate to their task or to their colleagues.

e The degree to which people:
- believe in consensus
- put work at the centre of their lives
- expect managers to use intuition.

2 In the following pairs of contrasting statements, say which dimension is being exemplified:

A: That was a very useful discussion, Nick, we've made a lot of progress. Thanks for coming.
B: I don't care how you do it, just let me have the results. I'm busy too, you know.

A: It's up to me. I'm going to get this contract signed before the end of the week, whatever else happens.
B: We don't seem to be pulling together. Perhaps some of our support team have been pressurised by this project.

A: She's the boss, so what she says is fine by me.
B: I'm going to have a word with my manager to say why I think that isn't reasonable.

A: We'll have to look carefully at this plan. It has implications for our investment programme.
B: We'll get some quick returns out of this, especially if we put a lot of money into it.

A: This is a very unconventional approach. It will put us under a lot of strain, and we have no guarantee it will work.
B: We haven't done this before, certainly there are a few risks, but it's a great opportunity to break new ground.

Aims
- To understand the principles of the Fons Trompenaars model for describing corporate cultures.
- To illustrate attitudes and behaviour typical of the different dimensions of this model.

Procedure

1 Ask students for any experiences they have of working in different companies or organisations where things were done very differently. Try to introduce some of the items from the activity, such as whether individual or group attitudes are prevalent (2, a), things are done in sequence or all together (7, c), and ask how this changes the atmosphere or culture of an organisation.

2 Introduce task 1, checking understanding of words and of the matching process. Encourage pairs or groups to start with the more accessible items such as 2 or 7, and to collect from their experience examples of some of the characteristics described. Ask for feedback and discussion, reconciling any differences and comparing examples.

3 Task 2 gives practice in identifying types of language and behaviour typical of the Trompenaars dimensions. Answers are suggested below, but use points of disagreement as a basis for discussion.

Outcomes

1
1 f, 2 a, 3 g, 4 e, 5 b, 6 d, 7 c

2
A Individualism / communitarianism (2, a)
B Specific/diffuse (3, g)
C Neutrality / affectivity (4, e)
D Achieved status / ascribed status (6, d)
E Sequential time / synchronic time (7, c)
F Inner-directed / outer-directed (5, b)
G Universalism / particularism (1, f)

Development

This would be a good time to explain a little more about the Trompenaars model (see Further reading below).

Linked activities

4.1, 4.2, 4.8

Further reading

Details on Trompenaars' system of characterising cultures are in

Riding the Waves of Culture: Understanding Diversity in Global Business, by Alfons Trompenaars, Charles Hampden-Turner and Fons Trompenaars, 1997, New York: McGraw-Hill.

Background briefing

Fons Trompenaars' first encounters with multiculturalism took place at home: he is the son of a French mother and a Dutch father. His lifelong study of cultural differences in organisational structure grew from these beginnings. Academically, these studies peaked in his doctoral dissertation at the Wharton School, University of Pennsylvania entitled 'The organisation of meaning and the meaning of organisation', which focused on the way culture affects how we perceive organisational structures. Professionally, he has been active as a consultant and trainer, and in 1989 he founded the Center for International Business Studies, which is now known as the Trompenaars Hampden-Turner, and is based in Amsterdam and Boston, USA. As an economist by training and a multiculturalist by nature, Trompenaars' work has focused on the interface of corporate and national cultures, particularly on how the reconciliation of cultural differences within organisations can lead to competitive advantage. He has posited a series of dimensions in which cultures differ. To those identified by Hofstede, Trompenaars adds:
- Universalism vs. particularism (rules vs. relationships)
- Specific vs. diffuse (correlating to Hall's low vs. high context)
- Neutrality vs. affectivity (concealing vs. displaying emotions)
- Achieved status vs. ascribed status (who you are vs. what you do).

These dimensions are described in his (co-written) book, *Riding the Waves of Culture: Understanding Cultural Diversity in Global Business* (1997). In a more recent book, *Did the Pedestrian Die?* (2002), he explores in depth the phenomena of universalism and particularism. His most recent book (co-written) is *Business Across Cultures* (2003), in which he shifts the emphasis from knowledge of cultures to knowledge for cultures by providing a new conceptual framework for dealing with the business implications of culture.

4.5 The Trompenaars model

Fons Trompenaars, in his book *Riding the Waves of Culture*, uses seven dimensions to describe different corporate cultures. The dimensions are shown below (1–7).

1 For each one, select the pair of contrasting characteristics (a–g) which best suits it.

1 Universalism / particularism	**a** Personal qualities and originality *or* loyalty and duties to the group
2 Individualism / communitarianism	**b** Controlling and directing your environment *or* being influenced by it and coordinating it
3 Specific / diffuse	**c** Doing things one by one, step by step *or* doing things all at the same time
4 Neutrality / affectivity	**d** What you do is important and brings status *or* who you are and what your contacts are
5 Inner-directed / outer-directed	**e** Controlling your emotions in a professional way *or* showing them and becoming involved
6 Achieved status / ascribed status	**f** Following rules *or* believing in individual cases and exceptions
7 Sequential time / synchronic time	**g** Sticking to facts and data relating to the case *or* using general feelings

2 In the following pairs of contrasting statements about the way project teams behave in a company, say which dimension is being exemplified:

A
- Each team member is given a specific area of responsibility and a number of rewards to be had if he/she meets them.
- Rewards won by meeting targets are to be divided amongst the team.

B
- Brainstorming sessions are used as a way to get started on new problems.
- Each member is proud of their ability to stick to target times and results.

C
- Team meetings stress the need for discipline and self-control, even in stressful situations.
- Meetings tend to be noisy. Sometimes they are confrontational, sometimes very friendly.

D
- Talent is spotted quickly within the team and promoted to positions of responsibility.
- Reputations, based on background, social status and contacts, count for a lot when appointing people to posts of responsibility.

E
- At meetings all items must be concluded with a clear decision before moving on to the next.
- At meetings different issues are dealt with at the same time, often illustrating common elements between the different issues.

F
- Members of the team keep a low profile with outside bodies until the implementation phase.
- Members of the team work to change attitudes in the community and other companies.

G
- Decisions are often taken according to precedent and usual company procedure.
- Calls are frequently made for new solutions to what are often new problems.

Aims

- To explain the Mole method of showing differences between corporate cultures in different countries.
- To illustrate the use of this model to profile corporate and national cultures.

Procedure

1 Ask students for any experiences they have of working in companies or organisations where things were done very differently from what they had been used to. Then briefly describe some of the behaviours shown in the activity, such as whether leaders act more as individuals than as group leaders, or whether the company's structure and procedures are firmly fixed or flexible. Ask how this can affect the atmosphere or culture of an organisation.

2 Introduce task 1, going through the dimensions first and then the list of attitudes and explaining that each one is to be ascribed to one of the two categories in each case. Ask pairs or groups to work quickly and instinctively rather than have long debates about meanings. Ask for feedback and discussion, reconciling any differences and comparing results. If possible, collect from their experience examples of some of the attitudes and behaviours described.

3 In classes where students have experience of working in different cultures, ask them to consider task 2. Use any experience they have in an open brainstorming session, identifying the characteristics given in the activity. As always, try to relate their conclusions to actual experiences rather than to stereotypes.

Outcomes

The following are the most likely results in task 1:

Leadership style

1 I **2** G **3** G **4** I **5** G **6** G **7** I **8** I

Company structure

1 S **2** S **3** O **4** O **5** S **6** O **7** S **8** O

Development

Ask students to present and/or discuss examples of companies they know which exhibit some of the characteristics shown in this activity, and to decide whether they are, on balance, more individual- or group-based, and more organic or systematic.

Linked activities

4.1, 4.2, 4.8

Further reading

The Mole Map is presented in

Mind Your Manners, by John Mole (3rd Edition), 2003, London: Nicholas Brealey.

4.6 The Mole model

The differences between corporate cultures in different countries are illustrated by John Mole in his book *Mind Your Manners*. He uses two main dimensions, each with two contrasting poles:

Leadership style

- Individual-based, in which a strong leader takes initiatives and directs his/her people firmly along lines which he/she mainly decides.
- Group-based, in which a consensus is sought among the group before major decisions are taken.

Company structure

- Organic, in which loosely-defined roles and relationships allow things to develop in a natural, largely undirected way.
- Systematic, in which clearly defined roles and relationships mean that people know what to do and how to behave towards other people.

1 Look at the lists of attitudes below.
For Leadership style, say whether each attitude should be listed as being individual-based (I) or group-based (G).
For Company structure, say whether each attitude should be listed as being organic (O) or systematic (S).

Leadership style

1 Autocratic: taking decisions alone ☐
2 Bottom-up: employees talking freely to superiors ☐
3 Democratic ☐
4 Directive: giving orders ☐
5 All having equal rights ☐
6 Participative ☐
7 Believing in superiority ☐
8 Top-down: telling people what to do, without consulting ☐

Company structure

1 The company is important, not the individual ☐
2 Functional hierarchy: believing in the system ☐
3 The individual is important ☐
4 Personal ☐
5 Rational ☐
6 Social hierarchy ☐
7 WHAT you do matters ☐
8 WHO you are matters ☐

2 Consider a country in which you have some experience of working. Think of the working styles and workplace culture, and say whether you have found people in this country to have, on the whole:
- a leadership style which is predominantly individual-based or group-based
- a corporate culture which is predominantly organic or systematic.

Aims
- To explain the Hall method of distinguishing between two groups of contrasting cultures.
- To illustrate the kind of language and behaviour representative of these cultures.

Procedure

1 Ask students to describe any experiences they have of the way different companies approach time. This could contrast the one-thing-at-a-time approach with multi-tasking, and will prepare for the monochronic/polychronic distinction shown in the activity. Do the same with the slightly less black-and-white distinction between high context and low context cultures (see Further reading).

2 Introduce the activity, checking that the words are clear. Ensure that pairs or groups take decisions as collectively as possible. Ask for feedback and discussion, reconciling any differences and comparing results.

3 Ask groups to discuss whether any of these cultural characteristics are predominant in any cultures they know. Americans, for example, are found by many people to have a low context style, and the Japanese a high context style.

Outcomes

1 Monochronic   3 High context
2 Low context   4 Polychronic

Development

Ask students in small groups to think of situations in which the four characteristics given are significant: for example, when giving a presentation or introducing a factory tour, the presenter can use a high or low context style. Many students will benefit from the opportunity to illustrate these two pairs of styles, so groups could be encouraged to develop mini role-plays. The short extracts in the activity could serve as a starting point.

Linked activities

4.1, 4.2, 4.8

Further reading

E. T. Hall's writings are a rich mine of anecdotal examples of culture. He outlines his system of Primary Message Systems in chapter 3, 'The Vocabulary of Culture', in

The Silent Language, by E.T. Hall, 1997, New York: Anchor Books.

Another source for Hall's thinking is

Understanding Cultural Differences by E. T. Hall, 1990, Yarmouth: Intercultural Press.

Background briefing

Edward T. Hall is considered by many to be the founder of the study of intercultural communication. He grew up in New Mexico and worked on Navajo and Hopi reservations there, becoming a practical student of anthropology before going on to study it more formally at university. During the Second World War, he commanded an African American regiment in Europe and the Philippines; after the war he conducted research on the US military government administration of Truk.

These wide-ranging experiences with various cultures fuelled Hall's ground-breaking work in intercultural communication. His work in the human use of space, time and context has become the foundation for many further studies.

Space: Hall pioneered the study of the human use of space, called *proxemics*. In *The Hidden Dimension* (1966), Hall shows that human perceptions of space are moulded and patterned by culture.

Time: In many of his writings E. T. Hall discusses the way time is used to structure human experience. Cultures tend to be either monochronic or polychronic: in monochronic (linear, divisible) time, events are scheduled one at a time and this schedule takes precedence over interpersonal relationships; in polychronic time many things occur simultaneously, and interpersonal interaction is more important than being 'on time'. His most in-depth treatment of the cultural perception of time can be found in *The Dance of Life* (1983).

Context: In *Beyond Culture* (1997), Hall discusses the phenomena of high versus low context cultures, which to a large extent correspond with polychronic and monochronic cultures respectively. High and low context refers to the amount of information that a person can comfortably manage.

4.7 The Hall model

In his books *The Silent Language* and *Understanding Cultural Differences,* E.T. Hall distinguishes between two pairs of contrasting cultures:

High context cultures, in which people speak indirectly, show respect, and maintain harmony. They consider it rude to be too direct.

Low context cultures, in which people speak directly, and say what they mean without adding unnecessary details or formulae. They are suspicious of people who speak indirectly.

Monochronic cultures, in which people like to do things one at a time and in sequence.

Polychronic cultures, in which people prefer to do many things at the same time.

Which styles do you think are represented in these extracts?

A
I'm afraid I can't fit a meeting in today. This morning it's my weekly team meeting. Then I've planned two hours' work on the budget. I could see you tomorrow at 11 o'clock, between a visitor who leaves at 10.45 and a scheduled lunch appointment.

B
Do come to the point. I need to get back with a decision by four o'clock.

C
In the circumstances it would seem to be inappropriate to attribute more than a general description of those characteristics we will be seeking in our new employee.

D
Don't worry about the timing. Just come when you're ready. I have a few things going on at the moment, but I'm sure we can always squeeze in a discussion of your problem.

Aims

- To show the need to consider to what degree international companies can and should create a common culture worldwide.
- To give examples of such standardisation.

Procedure

1 Raise the question of whether multinational companies should try to standardise their company culture, and if so, to what extent? If necessary, give examples of dress, and forms of address, both of which bring in the question of formality or informality.

2 Introduce the activity, dealing with **a** first – the question of which things, if any, should be standardised, or at least checked for some degree of conformity. Ask groups to consider this, then report back through a spokesperson. There should be enough items chosen as suitable for standardisation to carry on and ask pairs or groups to decide what the decisions should be on each issue. For example, should it be recommended that all meetings and appointments should take place within a maximum of 15 minutes of the appointed time? This should lead to detailed discussion which groups should feed back to the plenary session. If possible, try to reach a consensus at both group and class level.

Outcomes

Try to get the class to negotiate a set of guidelines for a large multinational company – one based in their country or in a country chosen by them.

Development

The discussions above could lead to a more general consideration of how the creation of a common culture can be one possible result of the internationalisation of a company, and the advantages and disadvantages this can have both for the parent and for its subsidiaries.

Linked activities

1.6, 1.7, 5.6

Further reading

For background information on the issues of diversity and conformity in organisations, see

International Dimensions of Organizational Behavior, by Nancy J. Adler, 2001, Cincinnati: South-Western College Publishing.

4.8 Diversity or conformity?

Some international companies seem able to adapt their corporate cultures successfully to at least some of the different national cultures in which they operate. But the successful blend of these two dimensions is not always easy. The parent company has to face the issue of whether to encourage diversity or impose conformity.

The following issues are typical of those which may have to be faced.

Read them through and for each one decide:

a whether you think it is an issue which should be decided on

b if so, what you think the decision should be.

1 What dress to be worn on company premises

2 Importance of punctuality at appointments

3 Which languages to be used at official meetings

4 Level of politeness at meetings

5 Use of private telephone calls at work

6 What forms of address (Mr/Mrs/first name/family name?) to be used

7 Accessibility of managers to their subordinates

8 Flexibility of work time

9 Length of time to be spent at work

10 Issue of reserved car park spaces

11 Responsibilities and roles of spouses

12 Need for written confirmation of verbal messages

13 Use of email, including copying emails to other people

14 Need for social gatherings to complement contact at work

4.9 | Case study: A takeover

Aims

- To examine decisions that have to be taken by one company taking over another with a strong local identity.
- To advise on the best decisions to take.

Procedure

1 Ask if any students have been involved in a takeover, and if so what happened. Draw on any local experiences, especially of an international takeover, and bring out examples of despair, frustration, anger, relief or happiness.

2 Introduce the activity, which is based on a real case, and which has an international dimension. Check for understanding, then ask pairs or groups to go through the list and decide on their attitude to each item: at this stage, simply ask whether they would act on it or not. Go through the list point by point, seeing how many groups agree, and encouraging discussion.

3 Encourage groups to put together a short presentation of this case study, outlining the situation and making their own recommendations for an action plan for Eagle Foods. Some students may wish to do the same for Birch, although their side of the case will have been less well rehearsed.

Outcomes

There is room for flexibility, but the overall approach in the real case was to make heavy investment in machinery, to encourage production; and in marketing and public relations, to encourage positive local reaction. Major changes in culture involving company names, brands, personalities and working styles were very limited in the early stages, although they became increasingly marked over time.

Development

Students who are interested could write up this example as a short report, including final recommendations.

Linked activities

1.6, 1.10, 4.1, 4.8

Further reading

An entertaining book-length case study in takeovers and acquisitions is

Taken for a Ride: How Daimler Benz Drove Off with Chrysler, by Bill Vlasic and Bradley Stertz, 2001, New York: HarperCollins.

4.9 | Case study: A takeover

A Swiss multinational food company, Swiss Foods, has bought a large traditional UK company, Birch Confectionery, with popular brand names but rather old production plant. Birch employees and other members of the local community were opposed to the takeover, and are in fear of losing their jobs. Birch has strong links with the local community.

Imagine you are advising the multinational. Which of these recommendations would you follow?

> Invest large amounts in updating the production processes.

> Wait at least three years before you make any major changes.

> Launch a campaign to help local people and workers get to know your company (Eagle Foods) better.

> Promote a local manager to a position of authority in your company.

> Begin to use the brand names in your international product range.

> Reduce middle management in the local company, mainly through voluntary redundancy.

> Make sure local managers have as much contact as possible with your head office.

> Sponsor local teams and organisations.

> Make sure your managers make their presence felt in the local company by making regular visits and inspections.

> Change the name of the local company to that of your own.

> Find the people who were most opposed to the takeover and brief them on your plans for the future of Birch.

> Keep the local press out of the factory.

> Hold regular information sessions with the trade unions.

> Offer generous redundancy terms to blue collar workers.

Aims

- To illustrate different types of group culture.
- To examine group behaviours in different situations.

Procedure

1 Ask the class if they have any experience of working in two contrasting types of organisation, such as public and private sector, or even a voluntary organisation as opposed to a commercial one. Draw on this experience if it is available; if not, ask them to imagine what differences there might be between the different types.

2 Look at task 1, asking groups to sort the list into contrasting pairs. Start with the more obvious ones, such as public/private sector, leaving more difficult choices to the end. Explain that some pairings (public sector/private sector, for example) are very close, so students need not spend too long on fine distinctions.

3 Ask groups to compare results (see Outcomes), then move on to task 2, in which they have to imagine the differences between the different pairs. Make sure the suggested parameters are clear (they may add more if they wish), and ask them to draw on any experience in the group, or simply to answer the question impressionistically. Compare results and discuss.

4 In task 3 they should use some of the results from task 2 to imagine a more specific reaction to the situations given. Ask pairs or groups to choose two differing groups of organisation, and to imagine the contrast in their reactions.

Outcomes

Contrasting pairs   Company department / Project team; Finance department / Sales department; Head office / Local company; Parent company / Subsidiary company; Private organisation / State organisation; Public sector /Private sector; Professional association / Sports club.

Reactions   Although no firm answers are possible, the following may help as a starting point for discussion and for the task. Students can also discuss how far these are over-generalised and stereotypical views of each organisational type.

Company department: a known and usually accepted way of working and behaving; well accepted roles, regular routines, few surprises or changes.

Project team: short-term results require careful planning, regular adjustment to circumstances, dynamic approach to routines and roles.

Finance department: careful and conservative in terms of spending, control and auditing.

Sales department: keen to spend where this may result in more sales; responsive to the market.

Head office: formal procedures; responsible for records and uniformity, even conformity.

Local company: flexible, adapting head office procedures to local circumstances; bearing less responsibility for methods, only for final results.

Parent company: keen to enforce some sort of standard procedure, behaviour, and results. Could be paternalistic, cautious or restrictive.

Subsidiary company: may conversely be more active, inventive, keen on development, but – repressed by the parent – reluctant or even rebellious.

State organisation: can be bureaucratic, slow to react, cautious of innovation, keen to establish and follow routines, with an impersonal style of communication.

Private organisation: has more entrepreneurial spirit; attention to customers and to shareholders (if any), aware of profit motive and need for business efficiency.

Public sector: formal, transparent, accountable to the public, with clear reporting procedures.

Private sector: able to be more informal, dynamic, responsive to local and temporary situations.

Professional association: has a sense of shared values and interests which must be protected and fostered.

Sports club: local clubs can have a more informal, even minimalist approach to administration.

Development

The relevance of group cultures may be extended into the social area, in which students could compare different clubs or societies to which they belong.

Linked activities

2.2, 5.4, 6.1, 6.3, 6.6, 6.11

Further reading

For a focus on the various types of diversity in teams, see chapter 5, 'Multicultural Teams', of *International Dimensions of Organizational Behavior*, by Nancy J. Adler, 2001, Cincinnati: South-Western College Publishing.

5.1 | Group characteristics

People working together in a group tend to adopt distinctive behavioural characteristics. Some typical groups are shown below.

Company department	Professional association
Finance department	Project team
Head office	Public sector
Local company	Sales department
Parent company	Sports club
Private organisation	State organisation
Private sector	Subsidiary company

1 Arrange the groups into contrasting pairs, for example: Company department / project team. Give an example of each type, for example: Human Resources / China Sea exploration project team.

2 For each contrasting pair, identify the main cultural characteristics (the way the members tend to think and behave). Consider, among other things:
   • structure: hierarchical or flat
   • attitudes: paternalistic or entrepreneurial; egalitarian or authoritarian; cautious or daring
   • style: formal or informal; personal or impersonal; flexible or inflexible
   • communication: written or spoken; fast or slow
   • decision-taking: slow or dynamic; individual- or group-led
   • approach to other people: direct or indirect.

3 Choose any two contrasting pairs from the list. Imagine how they would each react in the situations below.
   a   A general call for cost-cutting measures
   b   Reorganisation
   c   A takeover bid for the organisation
   d   The appointment of a new manager or managing director

Aims

- To show how different cultural expectations can make project work difficult to coordinate.
- To consider ways of improving communication in project teams.

Procedure

1 Students can read the text in preparation for the class.

2 Ask students for any experience or knowledge they may have of the kind of situation described in the case study. If so, draw on it; if not, ask them to imagine what kind of problems could occur. Deal with any possible problems of understanding.

3 Ask pairs or groups to consider the task – how the project manager could improve the quality and efficiency of this kind of meeting. You may suggest they first analyse the areas of potential conflict: punctuality, irregular absence, changes of agenda, family commitments, different attitudes to paperwork, haste, bluntness, mobile phones – all in addition to the usual practical problems such as late delivery and change of contract. They should not try to ascribe any of these problems to one particular member of the team, but simply consider some of the ways of addressing the situation. Should they be addressed:

- directly or indirectly
- in the short term or the long term
- with individuals or with the group?

When groups have finished, ask them all to give a short summary of the steps they would take, leading to general discussion.

Outcomes

No single solution is desirable here, but encourage the groups to identify and deal with all the apparent problems as positively and sympathetically as possible. The members of the project have to carry on working together for some time!

Development

Ask students for other experiences of project work, and other potential sources of friction, particularly with regard to meetings.

Linked activities

1.9, 4.1, 6.1, 6.9, 6.11

Further reading

For a more in-depth case study on multicultural project teams (in this case, German–American), see

'Crossing the Cultural Divide' by Patrick Schmidt, published in *Consumer Goods* in March 2001, at http://www.agcc.de/resources or www.consumergoods.com.

5.2 | Case study: Troubleshooting

Read this short case study in order to decide what action should and could be taken by the project manager.

A six-person project team of a US construction company building a new leisure complex in south-east Asia gathers for a project meeting scheduled for 11.00.

The American project leader arrives at 10.55 to find two project members chatting outside the room. One disappears without explanation. The American and the British financial expert look at the agenda and add two new items, but nobody else appears until 11.15, when a Norwegian construction engineer comes in, only to say he has to leave soon as one of his children has a doctor's appointment. The American rings the two other members of the team, who say they are on their way. When they arrive, they don't have their agenda, but are fully briefed. Informal discussions begin, which the American interrupts, explaining they have a lot to do in a short time. The first item on the agenda is the date of arrival of a major piece of equipment – an earth-moving machine – from the US. The news is that there has been a further delay. Secondly, the client has changed some of the requirements: the complex must be ready one week earlier than agreed in the contract. The British member's mobile phone rings, and she starts a conversation about the budget in the corner of the room.

Suggest what actions could be taken to improve the quality and the usefulness of this kind of meeting.

5.3 | SWOT analysis

Aims
- To examine the challenges of international project work.
- To show how these can be seen both as opportunities and as threats.

Procedure

1 Students can read the text in preparation for the class.

2 Make sure students are familiar with the concept of SWOT analysis, and if not, explain the principles. Ask if anyone has experience of project work – short periods of work with a team entrusted with a specific purpose, a budget and personnel. If so, share it; if not, ask for ideas as to what project work would involve for its members.

3 Form pairs or groups to pool ideas on the task. Students should be encouraged to identify as many new challenges as possible faced by Robert, and to view them from as many angles as possible. Most of the challenges could be seen as both positive and negative, depending on the way they are approached.

The following suggestions may help as a basis for discussion:

New working styles: more flexible, dynamic *or* stressful and time-consuming

Mixed nationalities: ability to compare different working styles *or* misunderstandings, time needed to adapt

Different working backgrounds of colleagues: stimulating new areas of knowledge from specialists *or* difficult to keep up with and coordinate with

Short-term work: will need to adjust, then readjust *or* may offer new opportunities for work

Short time to act: hurried, stressful, may sacrifice quality for speed *or* new dynamic work ethic

Frequent travel: see new places, faces *or* tiring; hotels and airports can be boring places

Regular contact with clients: expand experience of job, meet interesting people, constant socialising *or* getting to know people can be tiring and disruptive

New locations: stimulating places, lots to talk about *or* bewildering mixture is destabilising

Communication: may learn something of new languages and communication skills *or* several languages, little time available

Family life: exciting travel for family *or* possible disruption to children's education; would the family move to join him?

Outcomes

Student feedback could take the form of a short group presentation, including recommendations for Robert on how to make the most of the experience by keeping the weaknesses/threats to a minimum, and maximising the strengths/opportunities, both before he takes up the job, and while he is doing it.

Development

Discussion could move on to other ways in which internationalisation could change people's lives, such as enforced movement disrupting family lives as well as giving valuable personal and professional experience.

Linked activities

1.6, 1.10, 4.8, 5.1, 6.1

Further reading

Cultural difference can be perceived both as a strength and as a weakness. See pp. 609–31, 'Attitudes toward the culturally different: the role of intercultural communication barriers, affective responses, consensual stereotypes, and perceived threat', in

International Journal of Intercultural Relations, Vol. 26, No. 6, by J. Spencer-Rogers and T. McGovern, November 2002.

5.3 SWOT analysis

For any project team, it is possible to identify on the one hand a number of **strengths** and **opportunities**; and on the other hand **weaknesses** and corresponding **threats** to it.

An individual joining a project team from a more traditional form of organisation will face many new challenges. Some of these challenges can be seen either as a strength/opportunity, or as a weakness/threat. Some may be both.

The following situation is typical of those faced by a project worker.

Robert, a mechanical engineer from Mozambique working for a large petroleum company, is 35, married with two children. His company offers him a new contract as transportation coordinator in a multinational eight-person team reviewing and improving logistics worldwide:

- *all members are international specialists, two are academics*
- *9–12 month project, good salary*
- *extensive interviewing of internal and external clients*
- *based in Holland, with regular travel to Brazil, Papua New Guinea, New Zealand, Colombia*
- *quick set-up, quick close-down of project after publication of results*

Consider the challenges he faces and say in what ways they can be considered as strengths or opportunities, and in what ways as weaknesses or threats.

S	W
O	T

5.4 | Group perceptions

Aims

• To examine group perceptions of other groups.
• To show how these differ from the groups' perceptions of themselves.

Procedure

1 Without encouraging stereotypes, ask students if they have any views of 'typical' members of groups, especially of members of certain company departments. They may come up with stern or dry finance people, woolly or vague HR people, or studious, self-contained research and development people. Ask if these people have the same view of themselves, and what they in turn think of other departments.

2 Introduce the task, checking first that the list of words and phrases is clear, and that the departments mentioned are clearly understood. The idea is to visualise how one particular group views another. This may be done with a certain degree of humour, which could raise the question of stereotypes (see Linked activities).

An example might be:

Finance, thinking about Human Resources:
How do you see yourselves?	in control
How do you see them?	theoretical
How do you think they see you?	(too) disciplined

Human Resources, thinking about Finance:
How do you see yourselves?	very human
How do you see them?	dry
How do you think they see you?	(too) people-centred

Outcomes

The choice of departments, and the results themselves, will vary from group to group. One outcome should be that students see that the wide range of perspectives implies that no one view of people or groups is necessarily accurate or final.

Development

A natural sequence would be to continue the discussion of perceptions and expectations into the area of prejudice, and the misunderstandings and prejudice this can cause.

Linked activities

1.8, 2.5, 4.1, 5.1

Further reading

See 5.3.

5.4 | Group perceptions

People with different backgrounds working closely together can have very different perceptions of their own and others' identities and work styles.

Here is a list of attitudes and descriptions which members of one group might apply to another group.

aggressive	good at problem-solving	patient
cautious		people-centred
clear in expression	honest	precise
	human	punctual
determined	humorous	rational
disciplined	imaginative	reliable
dry	in control	slow
dynamic	ingenious	sociable
fussy	methodical	theoretical
good at handling large amounts of information	objective	undisciplined
	outspoken	vague
		well-prepared

Choose two of the following departments and list some of the different perceptions they might be expected to have of each other. Use words and phrases from the list above, and add others where applicable.

IT	Production
Public Relations	Marketing
Finance	Human Resources
Legal	Research and Development
Training and Development	Operations and Maintenance
Logistics	

Aims

- To assess to what extent written guidelines can help in defining desired behaviour in a multicultural group.
- To give practice in trying to establish norms.

Procedure

1 Students can read the text in preparation for the class.

2 Ask students for any examples they may have of cross-cultural friction, from their work or leisure experience. Ask if any of these could have been avoided by trying to agree norms of behaviour or communication beforehand. Establish that this kind of friction is always possible in multicultural groups, and that this activity examines the possibility of avoiding it by setting up norms.

3 Check that the sentences and tasks are clear, and ask pairs or groups to collate their responses. In task 1, students first give their responses individually, but then in their groups they can add together the scores for each statement, giving each one a group score. Ask groups to compare scores, identifying and discussing any major differences. At this point task 2 may be introduced, asking for alternatives for statements with which students disagree.

4 For task 3, brainstorm any extra ideas under either of the headings, business and social, and ask for comments from the rest of the class.

Outcomes

There are no fixed outcomes, but plenty of opportunity to discuss ways of containing a wide range of cultural behaviours even within a single code.

Development

Discussion can examine the legitimacy of this exercise and could then lead on to general questions about project teams. It is often commented that the human relations problems caused by the coming together of a disparate range of people can be greater than those caused by technical or practical problems.

Linked activities

5.2, 5.6, 6.3, 6.6

Further reading

For a handy catalogue of cultural conventions across the globe, see

Do's and Taboos Around the World, by Roger Axtell, 1993, New York: John Wiley.

5.5 Observing conventions

A multicultural project team which meets regularly both for business and socially may try to establish certain rules about behaviour.

1 Read the list of provisional guidelines below, and then put the appropriate number in the box:

5 = Agree strongly   4 = Agree   3 = Neutral   2 = Disagree   1 = Disagree strongly

2 Suggest an alternative to those with which you disagreed (2 and 1).

3 Add any other items you consider necessary.

Business

1 Arriving late for an appointment is unforgivable. ☐

2 A company's image is reflected in the way its people dress. ☐

3 Talk to all people as colleagues, not subordinates. ☐

4 Say what you mean clearly and directly. ☐

5 Interrupting somebody who is speaking at a meeting is impolite and counter-productive. ☐

6 Never say directly that you don't agree with somebody. ☐

7 Meetings should have a strictly observed timetable. ☐

8 Always explain to a colleague any doubts you have about their suggestions. ☐

9 Never disagree with a superior. ☐

10 Never say 'no' to a request. ☐

11 Always ask for permission to speak in a meeting. ☐

12 Always offer to do something, even if you are not sure you can. ☐

13 Always pretend to listen, even if you are not doing so. ☐

14 If somebody offends you, always explain to him/her what has happened. ☐

Social

1 Dress casually for social events. ☐

2 Always separate business life from personal life. ☐

3 If you don't know what to say, talk about the weather. ☐

4 Never ask anyone their age. ☐

5 Men should talk to women differently from the way they talk to men. ☐

6 Only speak when you are spoken to. ☐

7 Never disagree with a suggestion about what to do or where to go. ☐

8 Make sure you pay for any food or drink you are offered in a restaurant. ☐

9 Always consult a guest about what they would like to do. ☐

10 Use compliments freely. ☐

11 Don't discuss salaries. ☐

12 Employees' spouses should not talk about work. ☐

13 Never talk about colleagues. ☐

14 Always arrive a little late at social functions. ☐

Aims

- To examine differing communication styles within multicultural teams.
- To practise dealing with these differing styles.

Procedure

1 Ask students for any examples of occasions when, in a multicultural group, they have been surprised by what a colleague has said, or how they have behaved. There should be no shortage of examples, some of them humorous.

2 In task 1, ask pairs or groups to read the cases, discussing and if possible agreeing on, their choice of the best reply. There is again scope for humour here, perhaps with some mimicry of the more inappropriate responses. Collect feedback and see if there is any degree of agreement.

3 Move on to task 2. Collect responses and discuss the advantages and disadvantages of each. Students could be encouraged to role-play some of the situations, which again offer scope for humour.

Outcomes

In task 1, responses will vary, but usually at least one response will seem more sensible than the others. In task 2, aspects of behaviour will also be brought in.

Development

Allow discussion to develop into areas of flexibility and tolerance, and how these characteristics can contribute to good relationships, even if they are difficult to achieve.

Linked activities

1.9, 2.6, 3.2, 4.8, 5.5, 6.3, 6.11

Further reading

For more information on the role of culture in specific business situations, see part III, 'Business Communication', of

Intercultural Business Communication, by Robert Gibson, 2002, Oxford: Oxford University Press.

5.6 | Cultural dilemmas

The following situations are examples of what can happen within a multicultural team.

1 Imagine you are a member of the team, and select the reply you find most appropriate.

1 Together with a colleague, you are visiting a client in Rio de Janeiro. You have been waiting in reception for 45 minutes. Your colleague is angry and gets up to leave. You say:

a Sit down this minute. ☐
b Perhaps we should wait a little longer. He may turn up eventually. ☐
c See you back at the hotel. ☐

2 It's 11.30 pm on a Sunday. You receive a phone call from a colleague concerning next week's team meeting. You say:

a Hello, nice to speak to you. What's the problem? ☐
b It's rather late for this, isn't it? But what can I do for you? ☐
c This is far too late to ring me. ☐

3 One of your colleagues receives a phone call, but soon puts the receiver down in disgust, because his Greek colleague on the other end 'speaks such bad English I haven't a clue what he's talking about'. You reply:

a Yes, terrible, isn't it? ☐
b Yes, I know he's difficult to understand, but his English is better than my Greek. Shall I talk to him? ☐
c That's a narrow-minded attitude. ☐

4 Together with a colleague, you are making a sales visit to an important customer. Your colleague turns up dressed casually (trousers and sweater). You are dressed formally. You comment:

a You look very casual. ☐
b They're quite formal around here, you know. ☐
c We normally dress up for important customers. Do you think it'll be OK if you go like that? ☐

5 At a team meeting, one of your Scandinavian colleagues who you know has some very good product development ideas, fails to speak because Italian and French colleagues don't give her the opportunity. You say to the latter:

a Please listen, won't you? ☐
b Let's give somebody else a chance to speak. ☐
c I think Annika might have something to say. ☐

2 Imagine a suitable response to the following situations. What would you do and say?

1 A colleague has just given a carefully planned presentation on a proposed reorganisation. At the end, another colleague leans over and says 'Bullshit'.

2 Your team meeting is over-running. It is 17.30 and you have promised your partner you will pick up the children from their after-school activity. What do you do?

3 Your boss works so hard he never takes a holiday. He is beginning to look tired and is less efficient than usual. Do you say anything?

4 You have planned a conference in a hotel in the mountains. The main purpose is team building, although this is not explicitly stated. The instant reaction of one of your team members is: 'Great. My husband loves the mountains, he'll really enjoy it there.'

5 You have scheduled some regular team meetings for next year. One member of your team tells you he can't make it to the one in June, saying 'You see, in the first week in June I always take my mother to the coast.'

6.1 Individual characteristics

Aims
- To examine the part played by individual characteristics in a person's cultural profile.
- To exemplify different styles of communication, and relate them to cultural types.

Procedure

1 Ask for examples of particular styles of communication that students have observed in their daily lives or in the media. Encourage contrasts such as direct/indirect, formal/informal (see the list in the activity). Ask where these differences come from – from inherited characteristics or from the environment in which people live and work. Encourage discussion.

2 Introduce task 1, in which students have to put the list of words into pairs of opposites. Make sure they are familiar with all the words, and explain that some of the words are similar in meaning, and that more than one set of pairings is possible. Check the responses, including any additions, and introducing where possible examples of well-known figures who represent these styles. A suggested set of responses is given under Outcomes.

3 Explain that task 2 requires a little self-analysis in relation to students' own communication styles. In pairs, each student chooses five words from the list that best describe his/her style. Partners may be allowed a brief comment, but then individuals report back to the whole group on their results. Again, brief comment may be allowed, but avoid too much analysis as this could prove complicated and potentially embarrassing.

4 In task 3, ask pairs or groups to read the dialogues and ascribe describing words – about four or five words each, from the list or other sources – to each of the four styles. Groups then feed back their results, giving examples to explain their decisions, and discussing any disagreements.

5 Ask for views as to whether any of the describing words fit any specific national cultures. For example, do some nationalities tend to be more formal or more impassive than others? Draw on students' experience as much as possible, rather than on their impressions, and ask for examples.

Outcomes

Task 1: Suggested pairings
analytical/instinctive; articulate/reserved; atheistic/religious; cautious/impulsive; cooperative/competitive; direct/indirect; emotional/impassive; erratic/stable; extrovert/introspective; flexible/rigid; follower/leader; formal/informal; generous/mean; gregarious/loner; humorous/serious; listener/speaker; methodical/spontaneous; observer/participator; optimistic/pessimistic; proactive/reactive; quiet/talkative

Task 3: Suggested descriptions of styles
A – articulate, impulsive, direct, speaker, proactive
B – reserved, cautious, indirect
C – cooperative, extrovert, generous, gregarious
D – cautious, competitive, reserved, loner?, mean?

Development

Further examination of individual communication styles could be undertaken. Classes whose members know each other well and have confidence in each other could talk about class members; in other cases, discussion is best limited to figures from the media or from local society. Some radio or TV interviewers, for example, have a very aggressive style, while others have a gentler approach.

Consider also whether certain styles can be attributed to specific companies or professions as well as nationalities.

Linked activities

1.8, 3.2, 6.2, 6.3, 6.4, 6.10

Further reading

An excellent exercise for demonstrating the culturally determined values that underlie individual characteristics is 'Cross-Cultural Value Cards' and can be found in pp. 33–7 of 'Cross-Cultural Value Cards' in

Developing Intercultural Awareness, by L. Robert Kohls and John M. Knight, 1994, Yarmouth: Intercultural Press.

6.1 Individual characteristics

Individual characteristics may be inherited (due to genetics or 'nature'), or learnt (from the environment or due to 'nurture'). The following is a list of some of the words – nouns and adjectives – used to describe people and their characteristics, and particularly the way they communicate.

1 Arrange in pairs any words which are opposites or nearly opposites. Add any other words which you consider important.

analytical	follower	leader	reactive
articulate	formal	listener	religious
atheistic	generous	loner	reserved
cautious	gregarious	mean	rigid
competitive	humorous	methodical	serious
cooperative	impassive	observer	speaker
direct	impulsive	optimistic	spontaneous
emotional	indirect	participator	stable
erratic	informal	pessimistic	talkative
extrovert	instinctive	proactive	
flexible	introspective	quiet	

2 Choose the five which best describe you and your own communication style.

3 In these short dialogues, describe the types of communicator represented by each speaker: A, B, C and D.

1

A: OK, come on, let's get this proposal finished.

B: I'm not sure we have all the facts.

A: We've got enough to be going on with. We can always add a few more later, or work them out roughly.

B: Do you think that's accurate enough?

A: Of course. We'll go back later and adjust them if the client thinks there's any sort of discrepancy. Let's not be too scrupulous about this, we don't have all week to do it, you know. Everything will be OK.

B: Perhaps we should just wait a little bit longer?

2

C: Those sales figures for the new product range look pretty good.

D: In fact there are some of the old products included in those figures, so they're not quite accurate.

C: Yes, but on the whole they are impressive. The R & D people did well.

D: I should think so, with their increased budget. Anybody could do well with almost double the money.

C: I think it's impressive. Anyway, we're having a little celebration this evening. Are you coming?

D: Actually, I have quite a lot to do tonight ...

6.2 | Work types

Procedure

1 Discuss working styles (the way people work or seem to prefer to work) and ask for words which describe them. Try to introduce some words from the list.

2 Make sure the four work types are clear, asking for examples of how a person from each one might approach their work. Check that the list of words is clear, then ask pairs or groups to do task 1, selecting at least two for each type. Explain that different answers are possible. Compare results, asking each group spokesperson to explain why particular characteristics fit a certain type, and to give examples from their own experience. Suggestions are given in Outcomes.

3 Use task 2 as an opportunity for students to examine their own preferred working style. In pairs they should choose four words which best describe their style, then say which group they best fit. Colleagues should comment briefly with their own opinion. Each pair then reports back to the class, who may comment, again briefly.

4 Ask students to consider whether any of the given characteristics tend to be common in specific national cultures. For example, do some cultures tend to be more methodical or more creative than others? Ask for examples from students' experience where possible.

Outcomes

Task 1: Possible results

<u>Innovator/Explorer</u>
articulate, creative, innovative, impulsive, extrovert, instinctive, leader, proactive, spontaneous

<u>Checker/Regulator</u>
consistent, fair, analytical, cautious, introspective, methodical, stable

<u>Developer/Organiser</u>
articulate, far-sighted, methodical, optimistic, proactive, resourceful

<u>Adviser/Coordinator</u>
cooperative, enthusiastic, flexible, gregarious, imaginative, participator, stable

Development

Students may wish to discuss whether the type of work they do is the type they prefer. This may not always be the case! Consider also whether certain working styles can be said to be typical of specific organisations or professions.

Linked activities

1.8, 4.1, 5.4, 6.2, 6.3, 6.4, 6.10

Further reading

See 6.1.

6.2 Work types

People can be categorised according to the type of work they like to do or are best at.

Four possible categories are:

| Innovator / Explorer | Developer / Organiser | Checker / Regulator | Adviser / Coordinator |

The following words are used to describe the way people work, behave and communicate.

analytical	far-sighted	methodical
articulate	flexible	optimistic
cautious	gregarious	participator
consistent	imaginative	proactive
cooperative	impulsive	resourceful
creative	innovative	spontaneous
enthusiastic	instinctive	stable
extrovert	introspective	
fair	leader	

1 Select at least two words to describe people in each of the four categories above.

2 Consider your own qualities as a worker or as a student. Select:
   a at least four words from the list which accurately describe you
   b the category to which you most closely belong.

Aims
- To illustrate ways in which individual styles of communication can be profiled using a number of parameters.
- To relate these styles to different cultures.

Procedure

1 Explain that this activity is about identifying overall characteristics of communication styles, both of individuals and of cultures. Ask for the opposites of styles such as direct (diplomatic/indirect), inductive (deductive), and any others from the list, quoting examples.

2 Check that the sets of parameters and their explanations are clear, then introduce task 1. Form pairs in which each person identifies the description which best fits him or herself. Encourage them to use modifiers such as 'very systematic', 'fairly diplomatic', or even 'in the middle'. Partners should briefly express their reactions to the choices. Ask pairs to feed back the results for brief comment by the class.

3 Do task 2, forming small groups to consider how these parameters can be used to describe national characteristics. Explain that generalisations will be necessary (see activity 2.7, The bell-jar graph), so ask for specific examples wherever possible. In monocultural groups, choose both the common culture and one other. Multicultural groups should choose a maximum of two, to be decided by the group themselves. Ask a spokesperson from each group to report back, and compare similarities and differences in their respective reports.

Outcomes

Students should arrive at a short profile of their own communication style. Although the list of parameters is wide, it may be possible to add some more to the list (for example: loud, quiet, etc.).

Development

Students could present verbally or in writing a short summary of the prevalent communication style of a cultural group with which they are familiar: this could be a country, a region, a company, a profession, etc.

Linked activities

2.7, 3.2, 5.4, 6.1, 6.2, 6.4

Further reading

An effective training video that illustrates these points is

Communicating Styles, by Jeremy Comfort and Derek Utley, available through York Associates (www.york-associates.co.uk).

Communication styles

People communicate in different ways. Here are some sets of parameters which help identify communication styles.

1 ● Systematic – organic

Some people like to present information, or deal with topics, in a systematic, sequential manner. Others prefer to explore things randomly, relying on instinct or experience to help them touch upon the major areas.

2 ● Direct – diplomatic

Some people go straight to the point of a communication, with no time spent on introduction, preparation or formality. Others will spend time on social talk or on related matters before moving to the central point.

3 ● Formal – informal

Some people use formal and possibly complex language as opposed to a more relaxed, familiar and friendly style; the tone of voice can be distant or intimate.

4 ● Inductive – deductive

Some people make a suggestion or state an idea, then explain or justify it; others will present information first, then draw a conclusion or recommendation from it.

5 ● Head – heart

Some people rationalise and speak objectively and reflectively; others speak instinctively, following their feelings.

6 ● High context – low context

Low context communicators state the message simply and clearly, with no redundant material; for high context communicators, the situation, surroundings and other associated details are an important part of the communication.

7 ● Colleague – friend

Some people treat others as a colleague with whom they have a strictly professional relationship; others assume that most other people are their friends, and treat them as such.

1 For each set of parameters, select the characteristic that best describes your own communication style.

2 Do the same for another culture (national, corporate, etc.) with which you are familiar.

Aims

- To explore some of the factors influencing the communication style and cultural profile of individuals.
- To gain a better understanding of one's own profile.

Procedure

1 Ask the class what they think has made them who they are, particularly in terms of the way they communicate with other people. Encourage them to think of innate characteristics as well as traits they have acquired from the different environments they have been in.

2 Check that the language of the task is clear. Then ask students to do it in pairs, suggesting that they keep the question as open as possible, and using the guidelines where necessary. Each student should take about five minutes, the partner simply listening and asking occasional questions if they wish. Each student should then give feedback on his/her partner, summarising and pointing out anything they found particularly interesting. Ask for general comments as to whether students were aware of any strong cultural influences they had felt during their lives from any of the factors mentioned in the activity.

Outcomes

Students could prepare a short verbal or written summary of the points they have covered, describing their personal development.

Development

Students may wish to consider how representative they are of the national culture they belong to. If so, why? And if not, why not?

Linked activities

2.1, 2.5, 3.1, 5.4, 6.1, 6.2, 6.3, 6.9

Further reading

See 6.1, 6.2.

6.4 | Where do you come from?

In order to define some of your own cultural characteristics, consider the question *Where do you come from?*

Work with a colleague, and speak for five minutes on the subject. Interpret the meaning of the question in the way you think most suitable. Be as honest as you can. Try to cover some of the points below.

(Nature

Inherent personal characteristics, inherited at birth: emotional and physical attributes

(Nurture

Early life: general environment, family atmosphere, friends, school, social groups

(Education

School, college, university: the influence of teachers and colleagues, and of the subjects you studied

(Work

The influence of job, daily work activities and working environment

(Nationality

Any characteristics you consider fairly typical of your nationality, including any regional features

(Organisation

The culture of the organisation you work for

Aim

• To highlight different cultural perceptions of what should happen in a meeting.

Procedure

1 Ask students to describe a typical meeting they have attended, and any of the characteristics they remember, such as a high/low degree of organisation, formality or preparedness. Ask whether they think things are different in different companies or organisations, or in different countries. They will probably agree that the term 'meetings' can cover a very wide range of different events. Ask for anecdotal experiences of the strange things that can happen in meetings.

2 Check that the list of questions and possible responses is clear, and that students understand that they are looking for the most likely option or options, rather than a correct answer. Decide which national culture is to be considered. If all the students are from one company, they may consider the culture of that company. Do the task in small groups, trying to reach consensus. Ask a spokesperson from each group to give feedback, and encourage comment and discussion.

Outcomes

Groups covering the same culture should be encouraged to compare their results and discuss any differences. A short profile could be drawn up by each group of the meeting culture of their organisation, which could then be presented to the rest of the class.

Development

Students could explore other business situations which different cultures approach differently, such as negotiations, presentations, purchasing, appraisals or employment interviews.

Linked activities

2.6, 3.1, 3.2, 4.1, 4.2, 4.3, 5.1, 6.2, 6.3

Further reading

For more information, see 'Multicultural Meetings' in

Mind Your Manners (3rd Edition), by John Mole, 2003, London: Nicholas Brealey

as well as 'Communication Patterns at Meetings' in

Cross Cultural Communication: A Visual Approach, by Richard D. Lewis, 1999, Transcreen Publications.

6.5 | Meetings

All organisations have their own written or unwritten rules about what should happen in professional encounters such as meetings or negotiations.

Here is a set of options for the conduct of meetings in a medium-sized company. Select the options which best describe what happens in your own organisation or one you know quite well. If they are all possible, select the one which is most likely to happen. Add any other options that you think are relevant.

WHERE does the meeting take place?
- In a formal meeting room
- Around a coffee table
- In a restaurant
- In a private home

WHO takes part?
- Senior managers
- Anyone with experience of the subject
- A close-knit team

WHOM can you talk directly to?
- Everyone
- Those under you
- Anyone who has spoken to you

WHAT can be said?
- Anything you like
- Only what you really mean
- Only things acceptable to your superiors
- Only things acceptable to other participants
- Anything that will impress other people

WHAT can be discussed?
- Business only
- A mixture of business and social topics
- Social topics first, then business
- Business first, then social topics

WHAT OBJECTIVES do you have?
- Clear
- Regularly restated
- Never mentioned
- Hidden from some participants
- Clear from the context
- Referred to indirectly

WHEN can you speak?
- When given permission by the chairperson
- Whenever you like
- When the speaker has stopped
- During a natural pause
- After a silence of several seconds
- As often as possible
- Only when essential
- In strict order of hierarchy

HOW do you speak?
- In a low voice
- Loudly
- Using eye contact
- With physical gestures

WHAT TONE do you adopt?
- Confident
- Modest
- Humorous
- Serious

HOW MUCH do you say?
- As much as you like
- What is necessary for the purpose of the meeting
- The absolute minimum

Aims

- To understand how the conduct of meetings is influenced by the underlying behavioural rules of the participants.
- To develop a more sensitive and flexible approach to the behaviour of different people in meetings.

Procedure

1 Ask students for any particular rules they have observed in meetings, such as all remarks being directed to the chairperson, or participants holding up a hand in order to get permission to speak; or even to talk about experiences where there appeared to be no rules at all. This should draw out a wide range of procedures and understandings, some visible (holding up the hand), some simply understood (senior people have more right to interrupt). You may at this point discuss the relative merits of strict discipline in meetings, as opposed to a more natural, organic approach. There are arguments on both sides.

2 Explain that the task consists of holding a number of short meetings, in each of which a rule or convention is to be observed. Check that students understand the list of rules, and look at the list of topics. Form groups, ideally of five or six, and ask each group to choose a topic (they may take one of their own choice if they wish). (The topics in themselves are not of great significance here since the focus will be on the process.)

One member should be chairperson and one member should make sure the rule is observed, pointing out any failures to comply. Run the task once, and ask for feedback from a spokesperson. Get each group to have as many meetings as possible, applying a different rule in each one.

Issues which arise could include the level of politeness of both language and behaviour, the exercise of the right to speak and to interrupt, and the use of humour.

Outcomes

General feedback and discussion should focus on what it is like to have to remember and apply rules in a way which you rarely have to do in a familiar situation. This is a regular feature for most people new to multicultural meetings: if possible, draw on students' experience of such situations. This practice should make students more aware of what other participants are thinking and doing, and help them adapt to a given situation.

Development

Ask students to consider what for them would be the best set of rules to apply for an efficient meeting. This should raise the question of length of contributions, clarity of language and argument, the right and need to interrupt and clarify, and the need to avoid jargon which excludes certain people. This last point may lead on to the question of interaction between native and non-native speakers (see activity 6.8).

Linked activities

3.1, 3.2, 4.1, 4.2, 4.8, 5.1, 5.5, 6.3, 6.4, 6.8, 6.9

Further reading

See 6.5.

6.6 Following the rules

Rules of behaviour in a meeting are often followed unconsciously, and when different people have different rules this can lead to confusion.

Hold a series of mini-meetings lasting up to ten minutes with a group of three to six people on one of these topics:

- Technology of the future
- The lack of contact between people in modern society
- The separation of work and leisure
- Gender and work opportunities
- The effect of the internet on society

For each meeting, select one of the following rules and apply it firmly.

Rule 1

Before each individual can speak, he/she must briefly summarise what the previous speaker has said.

Rule 2

Each time a participant has spoken for more than 30 seconds, another participant must try to interrupt politely. The speaker must give way within 10 seconds.

Rule 3

If they don't agree with something the speaker says, participants must interrupt and express another view clearly and firmly.

Rule 4

After one minute of speaking, a participant must hand over to another person.

Rule 5

As soon as somebody says something which is jargon or too technical for colleagues to understand, other participants clap their hands.

Aims

- To discuss some of the advantages and disadvantages of English as an international language.
- To examine ways in which it can best be used as an international language.

Procedure

1   Ask the class about their attitudes to English, whether as their first, second or third language. Reactions may include a painful learning process, difficulties in expressing and understanding ideas, and happy experiences from social opportunities, travel and literature. The mix of both painful and positive experiences should be useful for this activity.

2   Introduce task 1, going quickly through the statements and checking understanding. In pairs or groups, students say whether they agree or not, and try to reach a consensus. Collect and compare results.

3   Introduce task 2, explaining that the intention is for the groups to try to decide whether each statement can be seen as an advantage for the language and its users, or as a disadvantage. There is no need for consensus here. Some possible reactions are to be found in Outcomes.

Outcomes

Some of the statements will be seen as advantages (its flexibility, its use on the internet) and some as disadvantages (its complexity, its colonial associations). Many, however, can be interpreted in different ways, such as its wide range of vocabulary, which on the one hand helps the expression of complex or sensitive ideas, and on the other makes it difficult to learn and sometimes to understand.

Sharing views and experiences on international English could lead to a more realistic and positive use of the language in an international context.

Development

Encourage the continued sharing of experiences of using English in multicultural settings, and discuss techniques for using the language constructively within certain limits, in order to avoid feelings of linguistic inferiority. Discussion of the role of the native speaker may come in here (see Activity 6.8).

Linked activities

4.3, 5.6, 6.1, 6.3, 6.5, 6.8, 6.10, 6.13

Further reading

For a general overview of the role of English, see *English as a Global Language*, by David Crystal, 1998, Cambridge: Cambridge University Press.

6.7 | Which language?

English is the world's main business language, and for at least part of the 21st century it is bound to be the *lingua franca* of international business transactions. But there is evidence that it will become less prevalent as the 21st century progresses.

The following statements about English as an international language all have their supporters.

Read the statements.
1 Say whether you agree with each statement or not.
2 Say whether you think each statement is an advantage or a disadvantage for international communication in general.

It is spoken by a large proportion of the developed world.

It is the language of the internet.

It has a relatively simple grammar.

It is considered to be a complex language.

It has a wide range of vocabulary.

A lot of people feel uneasy using it.

People from other language 'families' are disadvantaged.

You can make a difficult request very politely in English.

It is an old language, with many literary references.

It is the language of science and technology.

It is the international language of political, economic and cultural imperialism.

It is the language of international business.

It is being overtaken by Spanish in the USA.

There are more non-native than native speakers of English in the world today.

It will no longer be the dominant world language in 10 or 20 years' time.

It is a flexible language, adjusting rapidly to the demands of international use.

It is the language of the world's greatest economic power – the USA.

Other languages, such as Chinese, Spanish and Hindi, are growing rapidly in global importance.

English is used widely in all continents.

Aims

- To show how different attitudes and behaviours can be adopted by native and non-native speakers of a language.

Procedure

1 Draw on students' experience of speaking a language other than their own first language. Ask them to compare their performances in each language, and try to identify typical signs: nervousness, hesitation, apparent inadequacy in the speaker, and impatience and frustration in the listener. Usually the language in question will be English, but some students may have experience of another language being used in a similar situation.

2 Introduce the task. Make sure the list of attitudes and behaviours is clear, and ask pairs or groups to decide which of the five categories to place each one in. Ask them to consider implications carefully, as some of the decisions may not be as clear-cut as appears. For example, 'Asks for repetition' will obviously be typical of the non-native speaker, but it could also be a frequent activity of the native speaker who has difficulty understanding a strong accent. Although students should enter a number, ask them to be ready to explain details of this kind when they give their feedback: see Outcomes.

Outcomes

A few of the statements may be clearly typical of the monolingual native speaker (9, 11), or the non-native speaker (1, 16, 24), but many will be applicable to both (3, 6, even 8). Encourage students to see the situation from as many angles as possible, and to discuss ways of minimising problems or friction (see Development).

Development

Use students' experience of the native/non-native speaker situation to develop a discussion of ways of making both sides feel comfortable, including developing attitudes of tolerance, patience and assertiveness.

Linked activities

2.5, 3.2, 4.3, 5.6, 6.4, 6.5, 6.7, 6.10

Further reading

For a polemical viewpoint of the role of English, see *English as a Lingua Franca: Double Talk in Global Persuasion*, by Karin Dovring, 1997, New York: Greenwood Press.

Many international meetings are held in English. In such meetings some of the participants use their native language, others a language which they have learnt with different degrees of success. This can affect attitudes and behaviour.

Read the list below. Assess how typical the attitudes and behaviours in the list are of native speakers or non-native speakers. Put the appropriate number in the box.

1 = Very typical of native speaker   2 = Typical of native speaker   3 = Neutral
4 = Typical of non-native speaker   5 = Very typical of non-native speaker

1	Accepts decisions more easily	☐
2	Agrees with suggested agenda	☐
3	Asks for repetition	☐
4	Finds communication a problem	☐
5	Finds interrupting difficult	☐
6	Gets frustrated by breakdowns in communication	☐
7	Hesitates often	☐
8	Holds back even when he/she has something important to say	☐
9	Imposes decisions	☐
10	Interrupts regularly	☐
11	Is not aware of language problems	☐
12	Makes many suggestions	☐
13	Misunderstands the meaning of other participants	☐
14	Organises the agenda	☐
15	Reacts instinctively	☐
16	Reacts more slowly	☐
17	Sees few difficulties in communication	☐
18	Speaks fast	☐
19	Speaks slowly	☐
20	Spends a lot of time listening	☐
21	Spends a lot of time speaking	☐
22	Uses dense language and idiom	☐
23	Uses simple language	☐
24	Is over-sensitive	☐

Aims
- To show how communication can be improved by adopting a number of simple techniques.
- To practise some of these techniques.

Procedure

1 Ask students about the common causes of breakdown or difficulty in communication. It may be best to focus on presentations they have attended, in which problems such as lack of preparation, lack of structure, excessive length, and unclear speech meant the speaker didn't get his/her point across. Difficulties of this sort are particularly common in multicultural situations. Explain that in this activity, ways are discussed and practised of avoiding some causes of breakdown.

2 Introduce task 1 and go through the list of techniques. You may ask for additional items here or during their discussion. Groups should then decide on the usefulness of the items. The results will be subjective, but the important thing is to discuss and examine the different techniques.

   Ask for feedback from each group, collating and comparing results. Any techniques which are consistently ranked low could be dismissed.

3 Task 2 gives practice in some of these techniques. Encourage individual students to prepare a short talk on one of the suggested topics or another of their choice. They should each choose one of the techniques and concentrate on it. Alternatively, the topic could be dealt with by one group, with each member concentrating on one technique. The results could be amusing, and should lead to further discussion of the usefulness of the different suggestions.

Outcomes

Additional techniques could include:
- Make a strong start
- Explain and simplify jargon
- Put positive points before negative
- Be aware of the expectations of your colleagues
- Put simple things before complex

Development

The mini-presentation practice could lead to more general presentation practice, with particular consideration for the expectations of a multicultural audience and how to adapt to them.

Linked activities

3.1, 4.3, 5.6, 6.3, 6.5, 6.6, 6.7, 6.10

Further reading

Both observations and reflection are needed to keep communication open and positive in cross-cultural environments. How these skills can be trained is outlined in

The Art of Crossing Cultures (2nd Edition), by Craig Storti, 2001, Yarmouth: Intercultural Press.

6.9 | Positive communication

When intercultural communication is in danger of becoming confused or of breaking down, certain techniques may be useful. Here are some of the more commonly used ones.

1 Rank them according to their usefulness by putting the appropriate number in the box:
5 = Very useful   4 = Quite useful   3 = Neutral   2 = Not very useful   1 = Useless
Add to the list if you can.

1 Use good tone and tempo ⬭
2 Emphasise the positive more than the negative ⬭
3 Be human, show warmth ⬭
4 Ask lots of questions ⬭
5 Keep It Short and Simple (KISS) ⬭
6 Structure things clearly and logically ⬭
7 Summarise often ⬭
8 Use body language ⬭
9 Check that you are understood ⬭
10 Show that you are listening ⬭
11 Say exactly what you mean ⬭
12 Use humour where you can ⬭
13 Avoid sarcasm ⬭
14 Clarify any doubts you have ⬭
15 Look for signs from the person or people you are speaking to ⬭

2 Give a short talk on one of the topics below. Choose one of the features from the list (for example, being short and simple, and/or trying to include a little humour), and use it as much as you can.

- The corporate image of my company or organisation
- Genetic engineering
- Globalisation
- The domination of American culture
- Stress and how to avoid it

Teacher's notes   6 Culture and communication

Aims

- To focus on the variety of non-linguistic ways of communicating.
- To practise using them effectively.

Procedure

1 Ask students for examples of ways in which people 'send messages' other than by speech. The eyes are an obvious starting point, then other facial expressions and the hands. Ask for examples of good, effective practice and also of negative habits, such as constantly clicking a pen. Numerous anecdotes should be available, and the point should be made that different cultures regard these messages in different ways.

2 Go through the list of transmitters and receivers, and ask students to contribute more examples. They may suggest adding bad habits such as the pen-clicking mentioned above, or the slightly sensitive questions of touch (much more accepted in some cultures than in others) and smell, which although often considered a taboo, can – often unconsciously or semi-consciously – transmit strong messages.

3 Practise some of these features with task 2. Both members of each pair choose a topic to talk about (it could simply be an account of last weekend, or of a recent holiday) and communicate it to their colleague twice – each time in a different way. The first time should be with as little body language as possible, the second with as much as possible. Both partners then report back to the group how they felt about both versions. The second should be better than the first, but encourage students to be critical in cases where body language was excessive or unsuitable. The point should also be made that listeners/observers will have different perspectives on body language.

Outcomes

Students should see the effectiveness of appropriate body language, but should also realise that it should be adapted to the situation. Different cultures have different conventions in this area, both in terms of signs and gestures which are appropriate or not, and in terms of how much body language is desirable.

Development

Discuss body language dos and don'ts, including taboos, for any cultures with which students are familiar. Bring out the usual need for understanding of and sensitivity to counterparts' cultural backgrounds and expectations.

Linked activities

3.2, 4.3, 6.3, 6.4, 6.5, 6.9

Further reading

For more information on the interplay of para-linguistic communication, see part II, 'Cultural Dimensions', of

Intercultural Business Communication, by Robert Gibson, 2002, Oxford: Oxford University Press.

Multi-channelling

Words are only one part of communication. The body also transmits large amounts of non-verbal information. The sensitive use of all the different channels involved (kinesthetics) can increase the effectiveness of intercultural communication, both for giving signals and for receiving and decoding them.

1 Look at the list of transmitting and receiving agents, and add any more which you think are possible.

Transmitters		Receivers
Mouth	words	Ears
	sounds	Eyes
	variety/modulation of voice	'Sixth sense'?
Eyes	contact/avoidance	
	lively/dull	Others?
Hands	position	
	together/separate	
	still/mobile	
Arms	position	
	still/mobile	
Head	angle	
	still/mobile	
Body angle	facing/alongside	
Body positions	legs crossed/apart	
	closeness to other person	
Movement	none/gentle/rapid	
Others?		

2 Take three minutes to talk to a colleague about something. It could be about your present job, a hobby you have, or a group you belong to – anything you want to talk about. Do the same thing twice:
   • The first time, sit quite still and use as little body language as possible.
   • The second time, use lots of body language, as in the list above.

Ask your colleague to comment on his/her perception of the two performances.

Aims
- To show different stages of development in awareness of intercultural matters.
- To increase intercultural competence.

Procedure

1 Ask students about people they know with differing levels of cultural sensitivity. Discuss how the way they relate to people with different backgrounds shows itself (for example, lack of experience or refusal to understand, on the one hand, and beneficial experience and flexibility on the other), and consider ways of becoming more competent interculturally.

2 Introduce the task as being an attempt to define a progression in attitudes towards other cultures. Make sure the language is clear to them, then ask pairs to arrange the different attitudes in the most logical order. There is no fixed answer (although a suggestion is given in Outcomes), so encourage students to discuss different options. In the feedback session, discuss the desirability of different arrangements, taking the opportunity to discuss the reasons for each one.

Outcomes

Different versions are possible. This is one suggestion.

1 Monocultural approach – 'Everybody's the same really.'
2 Recognition of difference – 'There's something different about these people.'
3 Recognition of different types of culture – 'There are national and regional differences, and corporate and professional cultures, and …'
4 Realisation that most behaviour is culturally conditioned – 'There's probably a reason for this.'
5 Recognition of possible dangers – 'This could cause problems.'
6 Beginning to work on the study of other cultures – 'There's a lot to find out.'
7 Developing an interest in other cultures – 'This isn't as strange as I thought.'
8 Empathising – 'I see why they act like that.'
9 Trying different ways of doing things – 'This might work here.'
10 Learning by making mistakes – 'Oops, that was a bit of a disaster.'
11 Developing one's own style – 'I'm sure this should work well here.'
12 Becoming enthusiastic about cultural variety – 'What great potential!'

Development

Students could try to place themselves on the scale, or at least try to pick out attitudes which they feel they have. At the same time they could discuss ways of encouraging progress along the scale – simple measures such as travel, reading, and actively trying to meet people; or more organised measures such as courses and seminars.

Linked activities

1.4, 2.5, 3.1, 5.6, 6.4, 6.9, 6.12, 6.13

Further reading

For a collection of articles dealing with (inter-)cultural competence in a variety of environments, see chapter 7, 'Communicating Interculturally: Becoming Competent', in

Intercultural Communication: A Reader (10th Edition), edited by L. Samovar and R. Porter, 2003, New York: Wadsworth.

Developing intercultural competence

Awareness of culture, and competence in dealing with it effectively, takes time to achieve. Some of the different stages are listed in random order below.

Put them in what you consider to be the most logical sequence.

☐ Becoming enthusiastic about cultural variety ~ *What great potential!*

☐ Beginning to work on the study of other cultures ~ *There's a lot to find out.*

☐ Developing an interest in other cultures ~ *This isn't as strange as I thought.*

☐ Developing one's own style ~ *I'm sure this should work well here.*

☐ Empathising ~ *I see why they act like that.*

☐ Learning by making mistakes ~ *Oops, that was a bit of a disaster.*

☐ Monocultural approach ~ *Everybody's the same really.*

☐ Realisation that most behaviour is culturally conditioned ~ *There's probably a reason for this.*

☐ Recognition of different types of culture ~ *There are national and regional differences, and corporate and professional cultures, and ...*

☐ Recognition of possible dangers ~ *This could cause problems.*

☐ Recognition of difference ~ *There's something different about these people.*

☐ Trying different ways of doing things ~ *This might work here.*

Aims

- To examine different attitudes towards intercultural communication.
- To identify those which are most important for each individual.

Procedure

1 Ask students if they have any fixed views on intercultural communication. These views could be observations ('These people usually do this') or advice ('Always do this', 'Never do that'). See how much agreement can be found. It should not be difficult to establish that complete agreement on this subject is rare.

2 Explain that the object of this activity is to work towards a set of agreed views on intercultural communication, but that no two people need have exactly the same set. Task 1 is an introduction to some common attitudes. Make sure the language is clear, and ask pairs to decide on their own preferred versions. A few may be easy to agree on, but consideration will in most cases show the validity of each of the two different options. In number 1, for example, the meaning of 'deep down' is crucial: at a very deep level, everybody is 'human', at a higher level everybody is clearly different. So discussion should revolve around the issue of the level at which differences become significant, and how one recognises them.

3 In task 2, students should begin in pairs to compare their respective priorities, picking three (or more) statements which they consider important. They may modify or add to them if they wish. In the feedback session, pairs may give individual or joint conclusions, and results should be compared around the class.

Outcomes

Try to establish a class version of the statements. In order to do this, it will almost certainly be necessary to modify some of them; adding to them is also possible. The main objective, however, will still be to have a greater personal awareness of the issues involved.

Development

Interested students may wish to draw up a small personal 'rule book', or present their conclusions briefly to the class.

Linked activities

1.9, 2.6, 4.8, 5.3, 6.1, 6.9, 6.10, 6.13

Further reading

See 6.11.

Dos and don'ts

Rules about intercultural communication are difficult to establish or agree upon. People tend to draw on their experience to formulate their own ideas.

1 Read the following list of statements, and for each one decide which version you think is most accurate.

2 Choose the three statements which you think are most important.

I	Do / Don't assume all people or groups are the same, deep down.
2	Everybody has a very easily observed cultural identity, except / including me.
3	Gestures usually / rarely mean the same thing to different people.
4	If you say something very clearly, most people / few people will understand exactly what you mean.
5	If you look carefully at the face of a person who speaks to you, you will generally / sometimes be able to work out what they mean.
6	'Yes' means 'Yes' always / sometimes.
7	The best way to get somebody to do something is / is not to ask them to do it directly and politely.
8	Other people's habits are usually / sometimes really interesting.
9	If you understand another culture, you will rarely / still find it hard to get on with people who belong to it.
10	Many / Few people can operate successfully in more than one culture.
II	It is possible to learn most / some important things about a culture simply by reading books about it.
12	Communicating with clients from a different national culture is basically the same as / different from communicating with clients from your own national culture.
14	Always / Never try to make the differences in culture explicit to the person you are dealing with.

Aims

- To become aware of different styles of learning.
- To consider which styles may help in the development of intercultural competence.

Procedure

1 Ask students for examples of different teaching styles they have observed during their education and training; the younger the students, the easier it should be. Encourage humour if appropriate.

2 Go through the list of styles in task 1. They may not be familiar ideas, so take some time to make sure they are understood, asking for examples where necessary. As a reference, the activities in this book are designed to be largely experiential. Ask students in pairs or small groups to work through the list, and then to explain their decisions to the rest of the class (see Outcomes).

3 Ask students if either of the two types of learning can be considered predominant in their own national or organisational culture.

4 Use task 2 as an exemplification of how one of the two styles might be preferable in certain situations. In principle, where facts are to be learned, the cognitive method will have advantages; where understanding and attitudes are to be developed, the experiential has strengths. Elements of both will exist in all cases, but a suggestion of the more predominant style is given in Outcomes. Of course, one can debate how far these answers hold.

Outcomes

Task 1 This is a suggested division:

Experiential	Cognitive
Class talk	Autocratic attitude
Debate is good	Direction
Democratic attitude	Facts are learnt
Experimentation	Formulae are given
Ideas, suggestions	Mistakes are bad
Mistakes are part of learning	Student acceptance
Participation	Teacher explains
Student feedback	Teacher talks
Students work things out	Things are right or
Teacher devises learning	wrong
situations	

Task 2
Experiential: 1, 2, 4, 5, 9,
Cognitive: 3, 6, 7, 8, 10, 11(?), 12(?)

Development

Discuss students' own learning and development plans for intercultural competence, and see if either of the two styles is preferable in their plans. Help them if possible to identify sources of information and interaction.

Linked activities

1.5, 6.11, 6.12

Further reading

A rich mine of information on the interplay of culture and learning style can be found in pp. 201–15, 'State of the art article: A crosscultural view of learning styles', in

Language Teaching, Vol. 28, No. 3, 1995, by Rebecca L. Oxford and Neil J. Anderson.

Learning styles

Different cultures learn in different ways. Two broad categories of learning are:

Cognitive learning	**Experiential learning**
Learning by listening, reading and understanding information.	*Learning by doing, by practising.*
For example:	For example:
• Learning facts from a teacher or book	• Learning through dialogue with teachers and colleagues
• Receiving and absorbing information	• Developing knowledge or understanding through interaction
• Working alone	• Working as part of a team

1 Read the following list of learning and teaching attitudes and activities, and decide which ones you think are *cognitive* and which are *experiential*. Put C or E in the appropriate box:

Autocratic attitude	☐	Mistakes are part of learning	☐
Class talk	☐	Participation	☐
Debate is good	☐	Student acceptance	☐
Democratic attitude	☐	Student feedback	☐
Direction	☐	Students work things out	☐
Experimentation	☐	Teacher devises learning situations	☐
Facts are learnt	☐		
Formulae are given	☐	Teacher explains	☐
Ideas, suggestions	☐	Teacher talks	☐
Mistakes are bad	☐	Things are right or wrong	☐

2 Discuss which of the two styles – cognitive and experiential – will generally be more effective when learning about these aspects of a culture other than your own:

1 body language	7 history and geography
2 directness or indirectness of conversation	8 institutions and government
	9 politeness
3 entertainment customs	10 religion
4 everyday life	11 social customs
5 family	12 taboos
6 gender differences	